Prehistoric giants
the megafauna
of Australia

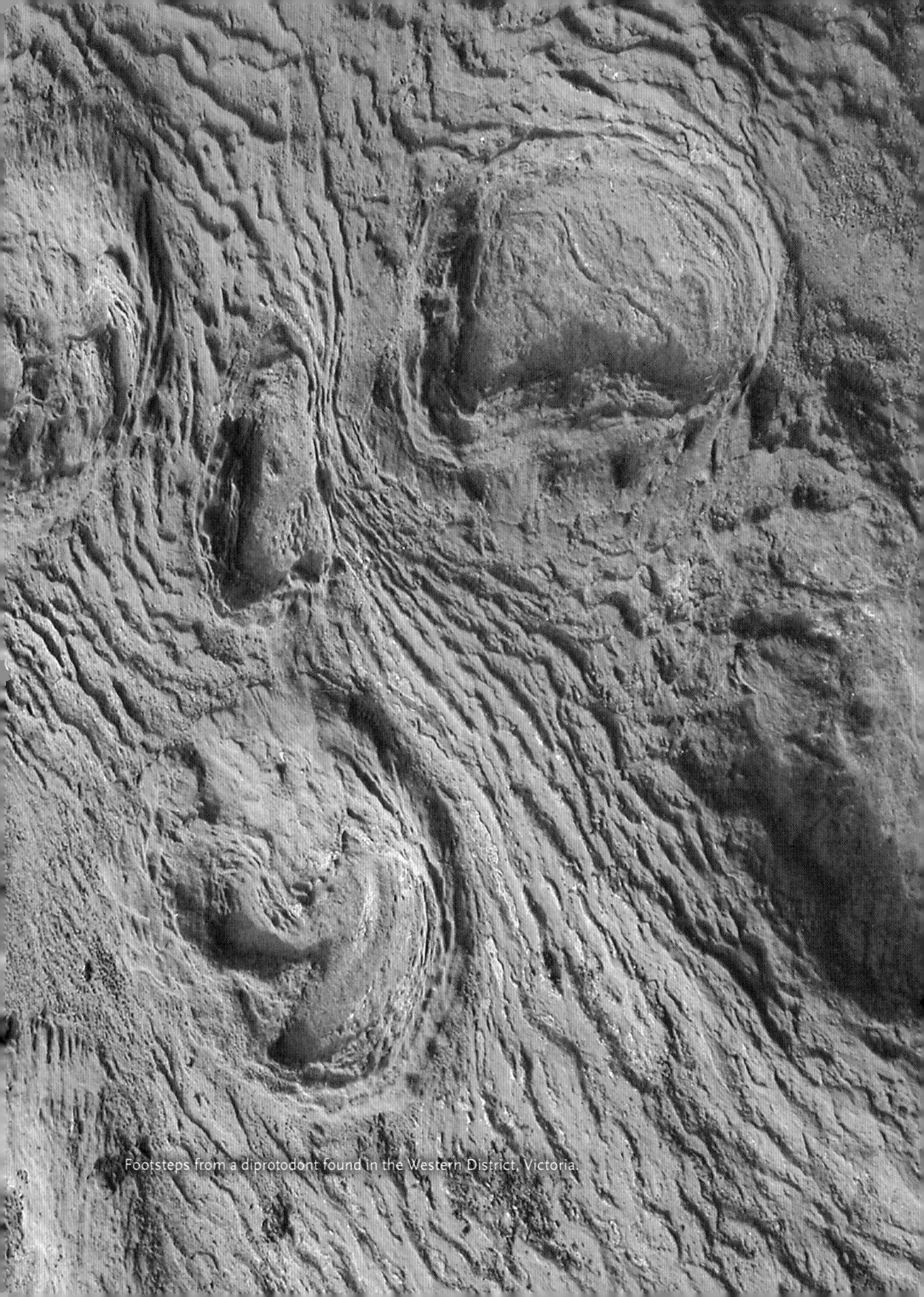

Footsteps from a diprotodont found in the Western District, Victoria.

Museum Victoria
Nature Series

Prehistoric giants
the megafauna of Australia

Danielle Clode

MUSEUMVICTORIA

Prehistoric giants:
the megafauna of Australia

Published by
Museums Victoria

© Text copyright
Danielle Clode 2009

Reprinted 2010, 2012, 2015, 2018

© Images copyright Museums Victoria unless otherwise noted. Museums Victoria has made every effort to obtain copyright and moral permission for use of all images. Please advise us of any errors or omissions.

Museums Victoria
GPO Box 666
Melbourne VIC 3001 Australia
Telephone: +61 8341 7777
museumvictoria.com.au

PRINTER
Asia Pacific Offset

DESIGNED & TYPESET BY
Stephen Horsley, Propellant

AUTHOR: Clode, Danielle.
TITLE: Prehistoric giants: the megafauna of Australia / Danielle Clode.

ISBN: 9780980381320 (pbk.)

NOTES: Bibliography.

SUBJECTS:
Animals, Fossil--Australia.
Vertebrates, Fossil--Australia.
Paleontology--Australia--Pleistocene.

DEWEY NUMBER:
560.17920994

COVER IMAGE
Megafauna Artist: Peter Trusler. This material has been reproduced with permission of the Australian Postal Corporation. The original work is held in the National Philatelic Collection.

'we live in a zoologically impoverished world, from which all the hugest and fiercest and strangest forms have recently disappeared'

Alfred Russell Wallace (1876)
Geographical Distribution of Animals, p. 150

Lord Howe Horned Tortoise

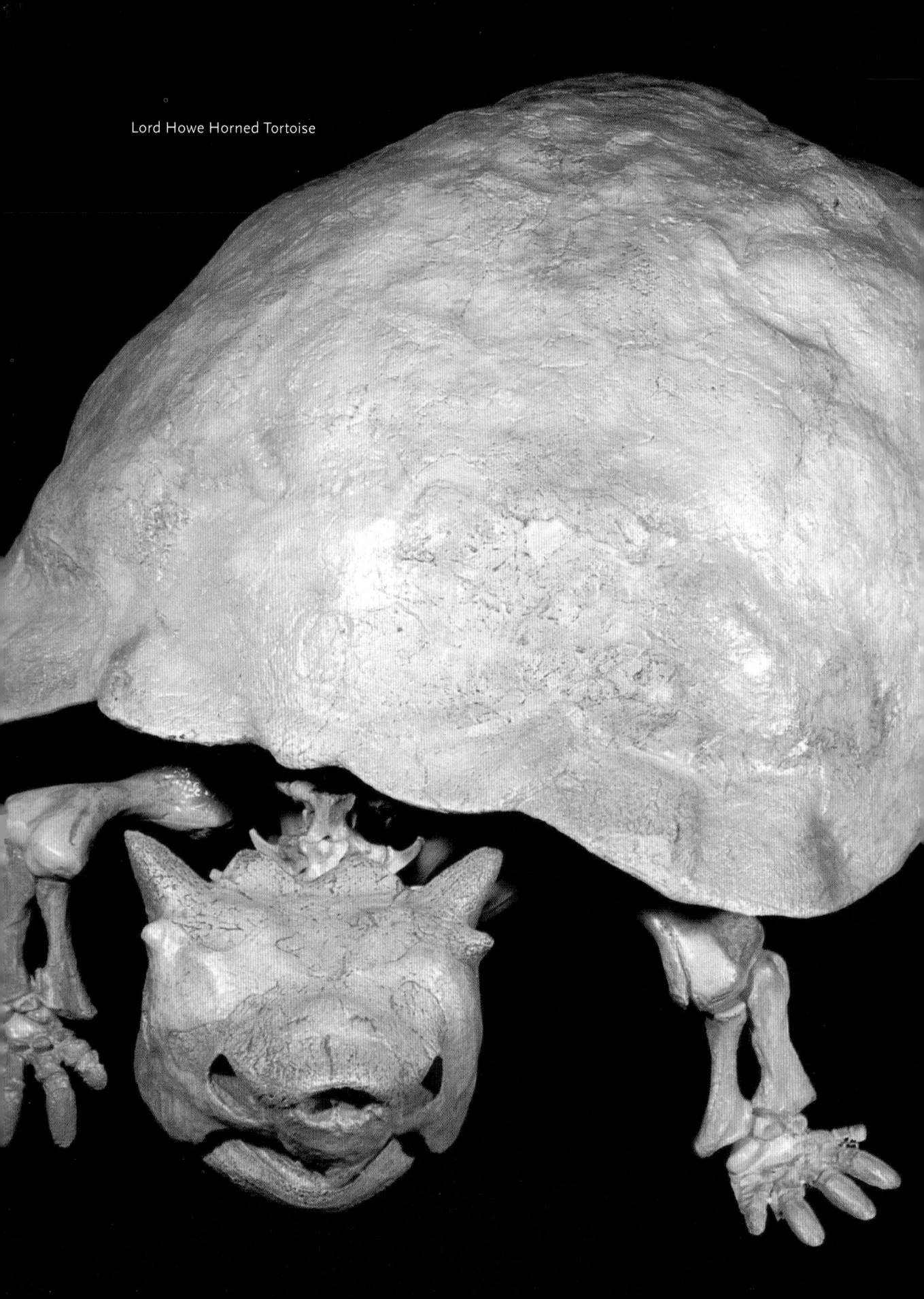

CONTENTS

Step back in time	1
Welcome to the Pleistocene	5
What are megafauna?	8
Australian megafauna	9
Pleistocene fossil sites	10
What do the fossils reveal?	17
The megafauna	19
Marsupial meat-eaters	19
Thylacoleo	20
Thylacine	22
Giant Rat-kangaroo	24
Cold-blooded killers	26
Giant Goanna	27
Crocodiles	29
Snakes	31
Tortoises	33
The big birds	35
Mihirung	36
Giant Malleefowl	38
Giant Coucal	39
Australian rhinos, hippos and tapirs?	41
Diprotodon	42
Zygomaturus	45
Palorchestes	47
Monstrous monotremes, wombats and koalas	49
Echidnas	50
Wombats	52
Koalas	54
Men of the forests and plains	55
Short-faced kangaroos	56
The extinct macropods	59
Modern kangaroos	62
Extinction	66
FURTHER INFORMATION	69
AUTHOR'S BIOGRAPHY	70
ACKNOWLEDGEMENTS	70

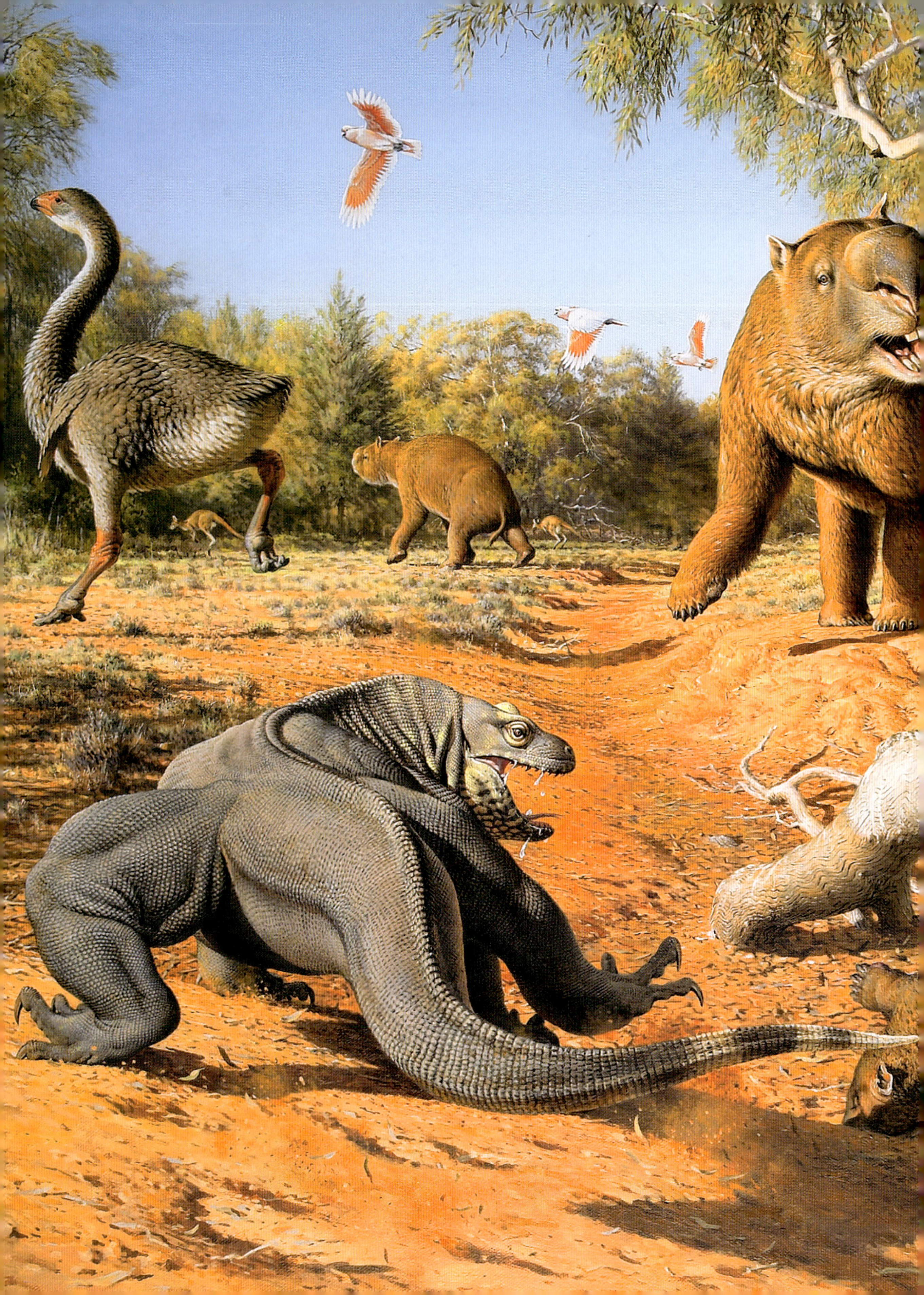

Step back in time...

Yellow eyes glinted in the semi-darkness of the early dawn. The thylacoleo sniffed the air impatiently, hoping for a scent of her quarry. From her vantage point on a low gum branch she could see nothing. Her short nose crinkled. Her lips drew back over long white incisors, as she drew in the crisp air. Catching no scent, she dropped to the ground and loped swiftly along the path of prints she'd been following for hours. The diprotodon was moving more slowly now. Perhaps it was old or sick. She quickened her pace.

The thylacoleo's two tiny young squirmed against the emptiness of her stomach. Soon, they would be too large for the safety of her pouch and they would emerge—miniature copies of herself, fiercely protesting at their expulsion. Soon, she would have to leave them in her den, just a few kilometres away, hidden beneath a fallen forest giant in the cool of the mountain ash. For now they stayed locked to her nipples, steadily drawing sustenance from her body as they grew. Her stomach growled.

The scent grew stronger now. The diprotodon had moved clumsily, breaking branches and leaving a wide clear trail as it went. The grass was wet with morning dew as the thylacoleo slid past, her sinuous yet sturdy body glistening and damp, her toes scarcely leaving an imprint behind her. With a quick shake she fluffed out her fur, barely pausing her steady advance. Small birds began their lyrical morning chorus in the cool air. The eastern horizon brightened with pink and gold streaked clouds. She would have to hurry. Time was running out.

Suddenly the thylacoleo broke clear of the low shrub, onto a rise. Instinctively she dropped to the ground, her eyes fixed on the scene ahead. Only her nose and ears moved, catching the slightest odour, the faintest sound, of her prey below. She backed away from the edge into the cover of the bushes. Creeping beneath a gnarled gum overhanging the edge of the bank, she leapt up its branches until she gained a clear, yet secluded, view of the scene below.

The diprotodon had stopped by the edge of a wide shallow lake, its path blocked by increasingly treacherous ground. A low grumble escaped its huge body as it swayed its head from side to side, confused and uncertain which way to go. It was alone—unusual for a diprotodon not yet fully grown. As it finally fixed its path to travel west around the swamp, the diprotodon tripped, stumbling under its own vast weight.

The thylacoleo's ears twitched. The diprotodon was lame. Slowly she picked her way through the shrubs above the lumbering beast. The slope to the lake was wide and exposed here—too far for her to run across undetected. Even a lame and solitary diprotodon was dangerous. She would rather take it by surprise. Further ahead the slope steepened and the swamp extended a long finger into the path of the diprotodon. The path around the swamp was narrow. The diprotodon would have to walk right beneath the vegetation overhanging the ridge above. That was her ambush point. Dropping back to the ground, she kept her eyes fixed on her prey and crept along the hillcrest on an ever-narrowing trajectory with the unwitting diprotodon.

The diprotodon lumbered on. It was confused by the swamp, which lay between it and the safety of the forest it could smell beyond. Its leg hurt. The diprotodon grumbled disconsolately to itself. Unaware of the yellow eyes following its progress, the diprotodon thought only of the cool green canopy which would shade it from the heat of the sun and the aromatic leaves it could snack on. Encouraged by the prospect, the diprotodon hurried around the last long finger of swamp that stood in its way. The thylacoleo quickened her pace too.

Just as the thylacoleo reached the promontory overlooking the swamp, the diprotodon stumbled again, its great weight sliding into a swampy pool. Now was her chance. Without hesitation the thylacoleo leapt onto the great beast's back, clamping her paws around its neck, driving her long, clawed thumb into its thick hide. The diprotodon bellowed in terror, raising its head to dislodge its attacker. But this was just what the thylacoleo was waiting for. Swiftly she struck at the soft exposed throat, locking her powerful jaws around the throbbing arteries and windpipe, crushing them closed. The great bellows of the wounded beast rattled and hissed as the diprotodon thrashed in the mud. Throwing its weight to one side, it tried to roll onto the thylacoleo, but she twisted out of the way, never loosening her vice-like grip on the diprotodon's throat.

The black mud of the swamp clung to the diprotodon's flailing legs, sucking it deeper into the ooze. A gobbet of sludge flicked up into the thylacoleo's eye, but she didn't flinch, hanging grimly on, one eye closed, as the thrashing of the huge body beneath slowed and weakened. Slowly, slowly, the body stilled until, with a last sudden spasm of its legs, the great beast lay silent.

Still the thylacoleo didn't release her prey. Sitting silently—unmoving—with her teeth bared and ears back, only her remaining open eye flicked back and forth across the landscape, always scanning for danger. After all the noise and struggle, the swamp fell strangely silent. In the distance, the small birds began their song again as the sun rose, sending its first golden tendrils out across the landscape.

After an age the thylacoleo shifted her weight, finding a more comfortable place to sit. Her teeth still firmly embedded in the diprotodon's throat, she retracted her claws and delicately unjagged her long thumbhook. Raising her paw, she awkwardly smeared the mud from her eye. Sensing no danger, she released her grip but quickly took a further bite, growling softly to herself as she moved. Twisting herself around, she scrambled off the body, breathing in its warm, moist scent of crushed eucalyptus. Sure now that her prey was dead, she let go, looking all around her nervously, anxiously.

Just as she was about to sink her great slashing incisors into the warm flesh of her meal, her hackles rose and a soft hiss behind her confirmed her worst fears. She spun around to face the megalania that had woken in the nearby shrubs. The reptile's long tongue flickered across its lips, tasting the scent of the fresh kill. The thylacoleo shrieked a futile warning. The huge old goanna casually raised its head, barely offering a threat in retaliation. Thylacoleo had no choice. Megalania towered over her and she was no match for such a large competitor, even a cold and sluggish one like this.

Yippering in frustration as she sloped back around the swamp, thylacoleo abandoned her prey to the great reptile. Glancing back, she saw the goanna rest its huge head on the diprotodon, allowing the sun's rays to warm its cold blood before it began its feast. The thylacoleo wasted no time heading back towards the safety of her den. When the giant lizards warmed up, the open country was no place for any mammal to be, even a large carnivore like thylacoleo.

The sun was heating the air rapidly, drying off the long grasses and releasing their sweet scents. As she passed, the thylacoleo startled a mob of short-faced kangaroos, sending the smaller females and young crashing off into the forest. The large male stretched himself to his full height watching the thylacoleo carefully. Aggressively, he scraped his claws across his broad chest, as if daring thylacoleo to attack *him*. But she was not interested. She thought only of her cool den now.

As she hurried on, a strange acrid scent caught her attention. She leapt into the nearest tree, clambering nimbly to the topmost branches. The smoke was coming from the east. Not from the conical mountains that periodically belched fumes, but from the wide flat plains at their base. Peering into the bright light, thylacoleo sensed that this was not a forest fire. This was not the roaring beast that swallowed up whole forests, consuming all in its path. This was not the monster that even megalania feared—not yet anyway. A thin tendril of smoke wound its way up into the pale sky. A camp fire. Humans. She would remember to avoid that side of her territory tonight.

The thylacoleo yawned, her jaws drawing wide and her tongue curling back. She dropped to the ground and headed into the cool of the forest and the safety of her den. Neither fire, nor humans, nor reptiles would disturb her there. Deep in the cool damp earth she could rest, until night fell again and she could return to her hunt.

Welcome to the Pleistocene

When the first people came to Australia they saw a very different landscape to the one we see today. Some of the differences were subtle. Sixty thousand years ago the Great Dividing Range ran down the east coast of Australia, just as it does today. A lush fringe of vegetation extended from wet rainforests in the north to tall eucalypt forests in the south. But this band of forest was much longer than it is today. The forest extended all the way from the highlands of New Guinea, across the Torres Strait, down the east coast of Australia, across the hills of what is now Bass Strait and into Tasmania.

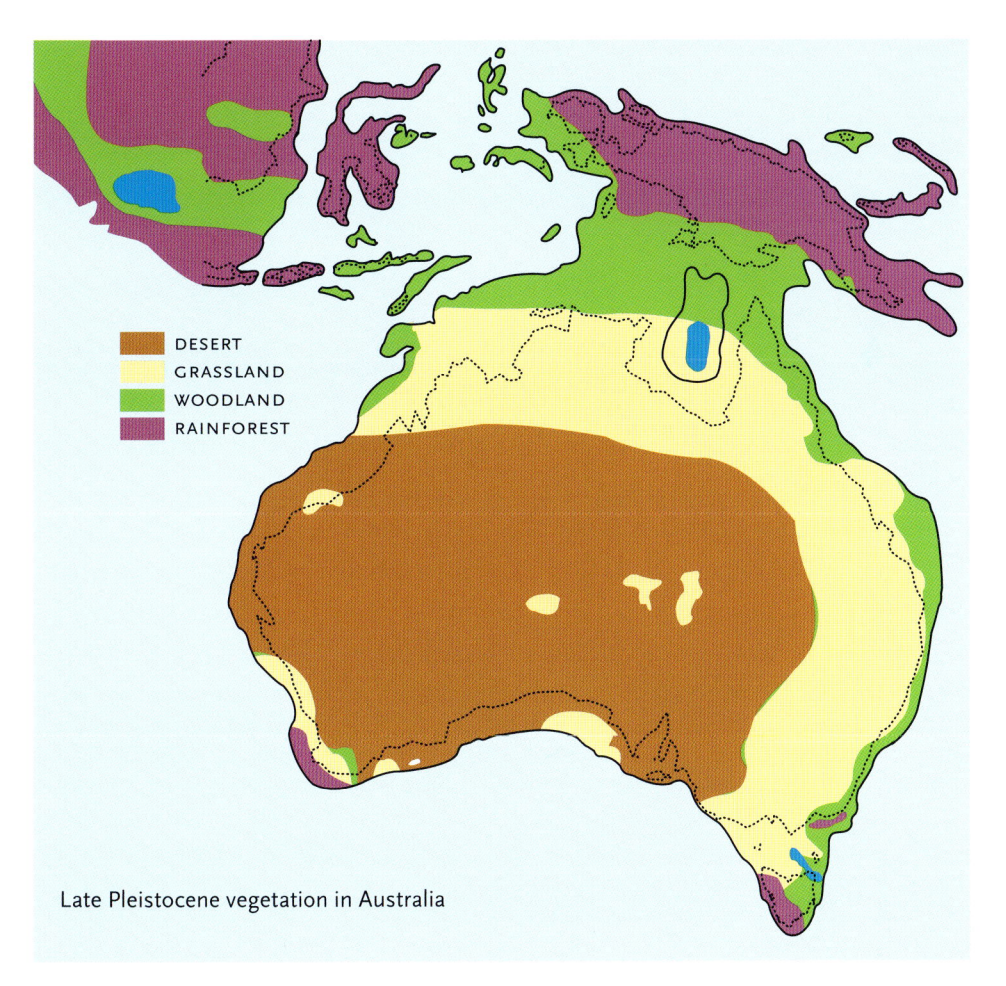

Late Pleistocene vegetation in Australia

Australia in the Pleistocene was drier in the central areas than on the coastal fringes, as it is now. But the cooler, wetter climate at the end of the last Ice Age also allowed a much larger area of open woodlands to flourish. Vast shallow lakes stretched across the inland, and the grasslands that now cover much of inland Australia had only just started to spread across the land.

In Victoria, changing sea levels meant that the coastline extended further south. At times Bass Strait was a low, wide, open plain. At other times it formed a shallow bay, fringed on each side by a row of hills and mountains that now form Flinders Island in the east and King Island in the west. Tasmania was not an isolated land mass, but linked to the Australian continent.

Shallow lakes and swamps covered large parts of Victoria. Volcanic activity pockmarked the region, creating rocky lava flows, scoria cones and crater lakes on the western plains. Periodic eruptions fired showers of ash and stones across the land. Great swathes of molten rock redirected rivers and created swamps.

Just as it is today, the climate was highly variable, with wet years offset by extended droughts. But change crept slowly onwards. The wet years were becoming less frequent; the rainfall was reducing. Cold, dry winds swept across the country spelling doom for many of the strange and diverse creatures that once inhabited our land.

The animals that lived in Australia in the late Pleistocene were very different from the ones we see today. The wombats, echidnas and koalas were gigantic compared to the ones we are familiar with. Vast mobs of kangaroos roamed the inland, but they were not always the same species that we know today. The most common species were giant short-faced kangaroos. The largest of these kangaroos was *Procoptodon goliah*, which stood nearly two and a half metres tall and weighed over two hundred kilograms—three times the size of a big red kangaroo today.

Impressive though many Pleistocene kangaroos were, they were dwarfed by some of their fellow herbivores. Creatures quite unlike anything seen today also browsed on the ancient forests. Diprotodons the size of small four-wheel drive cars roamed the countryside in herds. *Palorchestes* was a tapir-like creature the size of a large cow, which probably used its claws and powerful forearms to strip the bark from trees. *Zygomaturus*, another member of the diprotodont family, may have had a short trunk and could have been aquatic.

Perhaps even stranger still were the last of the mihirung, a family of giant birds most closely related to ducks. By the Pleistocene this once abundant family was represented by just one species—Newton's Mihirung, which stood only a bit taller than a modern Emu but was five times an Emu's weight.

PRECAMBRIAN

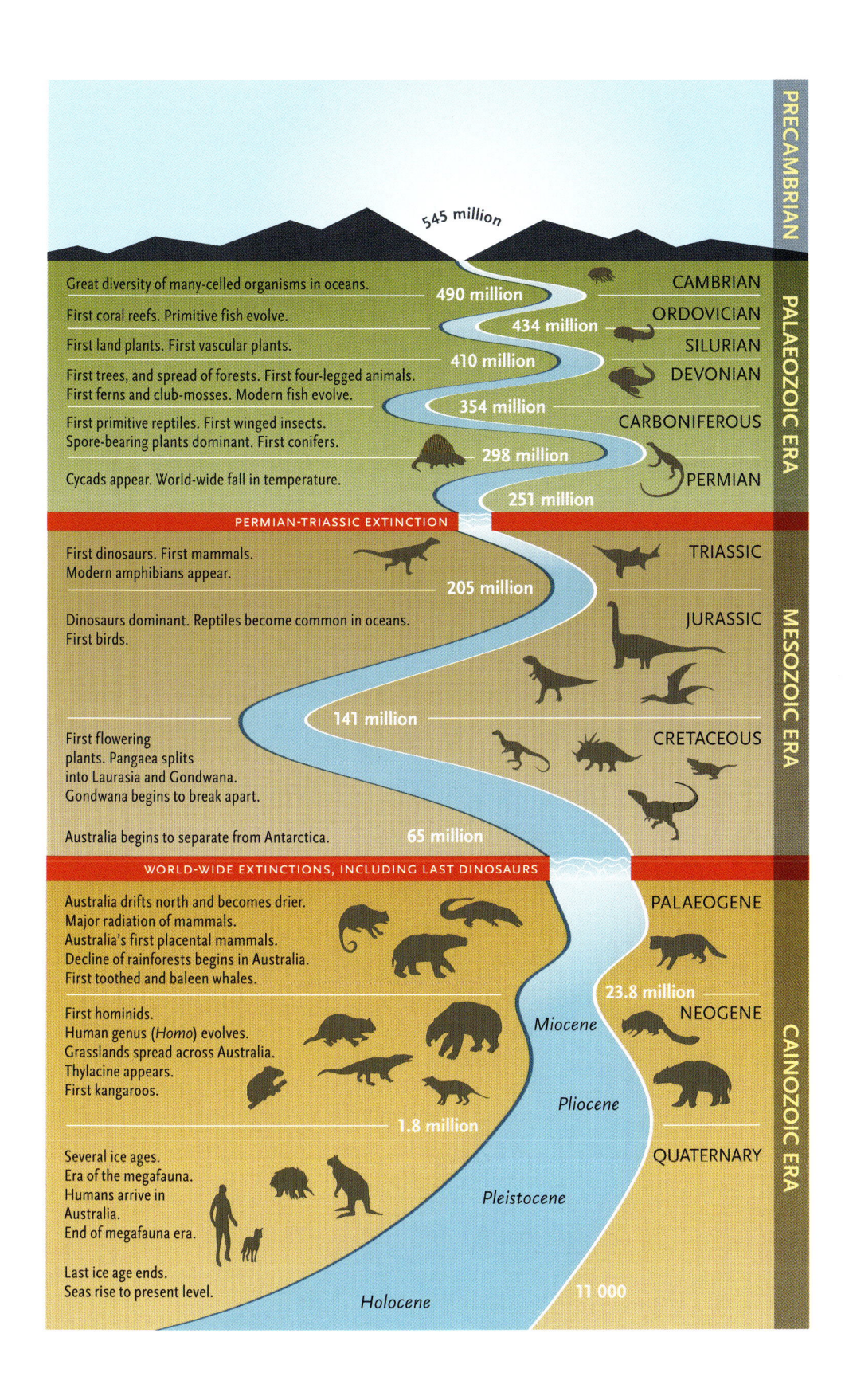

545 million

PALAEOZOIC ERA

Great diversity of many-celled organisms in oceans. — 490 million — **CAMBRIAN**

First coral reefs. Primitive fish evolve. — 434 million — **ORDOVICIAN**

First land plants. First vascular plants. — 410 million — **SILURIAN**

First trees, and spread of forests. First four-legged animals. First ferns and club-mosses. Modern fish evolve. — 354 million — **DEVONIAN**

First primitive reptiles. First winged insects. Spore-bearing plants dominant. First conifers. — 298 million — **CARBONIFEROUS**

Cycads appear. World-wide fall in temperature. — 251 million — **PERMIAN**

PERMIAN-TRIASSIC EXTINCTION

MESOZOIC ERA

First dinosaurs. First mammals. Modern amphibians appear. — 205 million — **TRIASSIC**

Dinosaurs dominant. Reptiles become common in oceans. First birds. — 141 million — **JURASSIC**

First flowering plants. Pangaea splits into Laurasia and Gondwana. Gondwana begins to break apart.

Australia begins to separate from Antarctica. — 65 million — **CRETACEOUS**

WORLD-WIDE EXTINCTIONS, INCLUDING LAST DINOSAURS

CAINOZOIC ERA

Australia drifts north and becomes drier. Major radiation of mammals. Australia's first placental mammals. Decline of rainforests begins in Australia. First toothed and baleen whales. — **PALAEOGENE**

First hominids. Human genus (*Homo*) evolves. Grasslands spread across Australia. Thylacine appears. First kangaroos. — 23.8 million — **NEOGENE**

Miocene

Pliocene

— 1.8 million — **QUATERNARY**

Several ice ages. Era of the megafauna. Humans arrive in Australia. End of megafauna era.

Pleistocene

Last ice age ends. Seas rise to present level.

Holocene

11 000

There were also plenty of meat-eaters to prey on these big herbivores. The marsupial *Thylacoleo* was similar to a leopard in size and hunting strategy. Carnivores such as the Thylacine and Tasmanian Devil were more common and larger than they are now. Some plant-eaters even evolved into carnivores. The Giant Rat-kangaroo, *Propleopus oscillans*, stood two metres high. Unlike its small, secretive modern relative, the forest-dwelling Musky Rat-kangaroo, this giant used its slashing teeth on meat rather than fruit, insects and fungi.

But the dominant carnivores in many parts of Australia were not mammals, but reptiles. The Giant Goanna, *Megalania prisca*, was the size of a small dinosaur. It grew up to six metres long and may have weighed over a tonne, making it bigger than most modern saltwater crocodiles. Large crocodiles were common in the Pleistocene, and included the giant *Pallimnarchus* crocodile of the north and the land-dwelling *Quinkana*. Giant snakes and strange horned tortoises completed this menagerie of Australian giants. These large animals of the Pleistocene are known as megafauna, and they were part of a cohort of giant species that characterised the Pleistocene around the world.

Most of the species found in Australia today were also present in the Pleistocene, but many were much larger than they are now. About 10 000 years ago, at the beginning of the modern Holocene era, all of the largest animals had disappeared. They either went extinct, or dwarfed over time into the smaller forms we see today.

What are megafauna?

Megafauna were large animals that went extinct during the Pleistocene, just when humans were spreading around the world. They were often similar to the animals we have today, but were a lot bigger. Many large animals, such as dinosaurs, went extinct much earlier in Earth's history. Other large animals, such as whales and elephants, have survived into modern times. But the term 'megafauna' refers only to large species (usually over forty-five kilograms) that went extinct in the Pleistocene. Of course many other small species also disappeared during the Pleistocene, but the 'giants' get all the attention.

Megafauna occurred across the globe. Woolly Mammoths and Sabre-toothed Tigers are the best-known examples, but each continent had its own legion of giants. In Europe, the mammoths grazed alongside giant rhinoceroses and cave bears. In North America, mammoths and mastodons co-existed with ground sloths and giant *Aiolornis* birds with wingspans of five to six metres. In South America, the armadillo-like *Doedicurus* defended itself with its formidable tail club against Sabre-toothed Tigers and three-metre tall 'terror birds' or phorusrhacids. Even islands had their giants, such as New Zealand's flightless moas and Madagascar's Elephant Bird.

Yet by the end of the Pleistocene, between ten and thirty thousand years ago, most of these large species had disappeared. The only large species to survive were in Africa and in the oceans, leaving us with Elephants, Hippos and Blue Whales. North America lost at least half of its large species while South America and Eurasia lost almost one-third. But in Australia, the toll was the highest of all. Nearly two-thirds of our largest species disappeared altogether. In a land where the two-tonne *Diprotodon* once roamed the open forests, today there is no native land animal larger than eighty-five kilograms.

Australian megafauna

Australia never had as many 'really big' animals as the other continents had. Perhaps our poorer soils could not support the larger herbivores that other continents could support. Nonetheless, Australian species show the same general patterns of increase and decline seen on other continents.

In the time of the Miocene, many modern mammal species first appear in the fossil record. These generally tended to be smaller animals. But, as time progressed these species often got larger, or related species appeared which were significantly larger than their ancestors. By the late Pleistocene animals in many families had become four times the size of those in the Miocene.

For example, the earliest diprotodontids were the smaller *Ngapakaldia*, which were perhaps only the size of a modern sheep or large dog. Later diprotodons, like *Neohelos* were slightly larger, but it wasn't until late Miocene that really large diprotodons started to appear. By the end of the Pleistocene the largest marsupials of all, *Diprotodon optatum*, had evolved. Similarly, the oldest short-faced kangaroo was only a little bigger than a small wallaby and yet by the late Pleistocene the family was characterised by *Procoptodon goliah*, three times the size of a modern Red Kangaroo.

What gave rise to this era of giants is unknown. What caused their extinction is even more contentious. For some species, we have no more than a few fragments of bone to deduce their original size, appearance and habits, while for

PREHISTORIC GIANTS: THE MEGAFAUNA OF AUSTRALIA

others we have a wealth of fossil material. But for all of these long-gone species the information is patchy and incomplete, and our image of what these great beasts must have looked like shifts and changes the more we discover and the more we study the little evidence we have of them.

Pleistocene fossil sites

What we do know about Australian megafauna comes mainly from fossils—fossils of bones, footprints, plants, pollen and other organic matter. Because the Pleistocene was not that long ago, dating these fossil sites precisely can sometimes be difficult. Some sites may have been disturbed or reworked in recent times, disrupting the layers scientists would normally use for dating remains. Other sites may have been exposed and damaged by erosion.

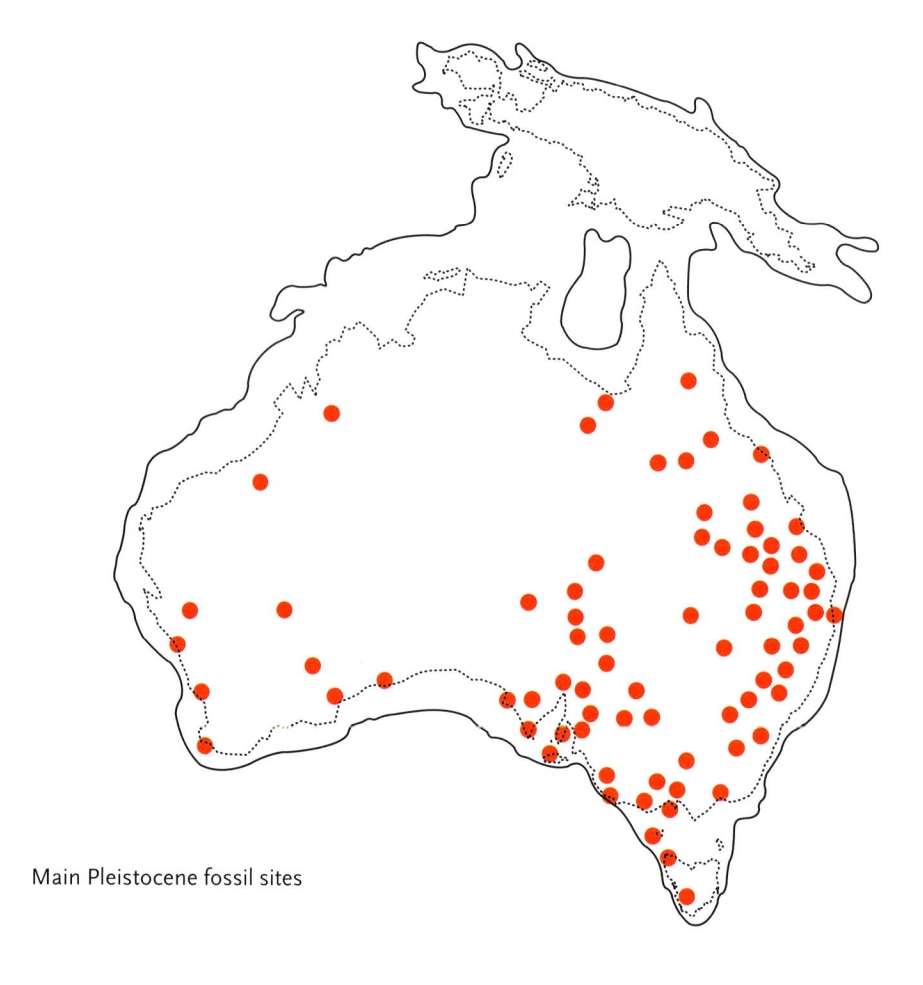

Main Pleistocene fossil sites

Pleistocene fossils in Australia typically occur in caves or surface features. Caves often form natural traps for large animals. Some sites, particularly in caves, provide a seamless collection of data from the 'fossils' of the Pleistocene to modern remains. There are many other less well-known sites where only a few fossils have been found. In some places, like Riversleigh in Queensland or the Buchan Caves in Victoria, Pleistocene fossils form only a small proportion of material from a much earlier time.

The Buchan Caves in Victoria

Wellington Caves

Wellington Caves, about two hundred and fifty kilometres north-west of Sydney, form a huge limestone cave system dripping with stalactites and stalagmites. In May 1830, farmer and rural magistrate George Ranken was fossicking in the caves. Like many educated men of his time, Ranken was also an enthusiastic collector of fossils. In one cave he stumbled across a bone on the floor and, looking around, he realised that the floor and walls of the cave were littered with embedded bones. Even the rock to which he had tied his rope to enter the cave turned out to be a huge fossil, 'the thigh bone, I conceive, of some quadruped much larger than the ox or buffalo, and probably of the Irish elk, the rhinoceros, or elephant'.

Ranken returned to the caves with his friend, the explorer Thomas Mitchell. They retrieved many bones which were sent to London and then to Paris. In London a young scientist called Richard Owen saw the bones. Owen would devote much of his later career to these strange creatures, so different from the living Australian animals. Over the years, Owen utilised a great network of collectors in Australia, ultimately publishing a book of his research into the fossil remains of extinct mammals in Australia.

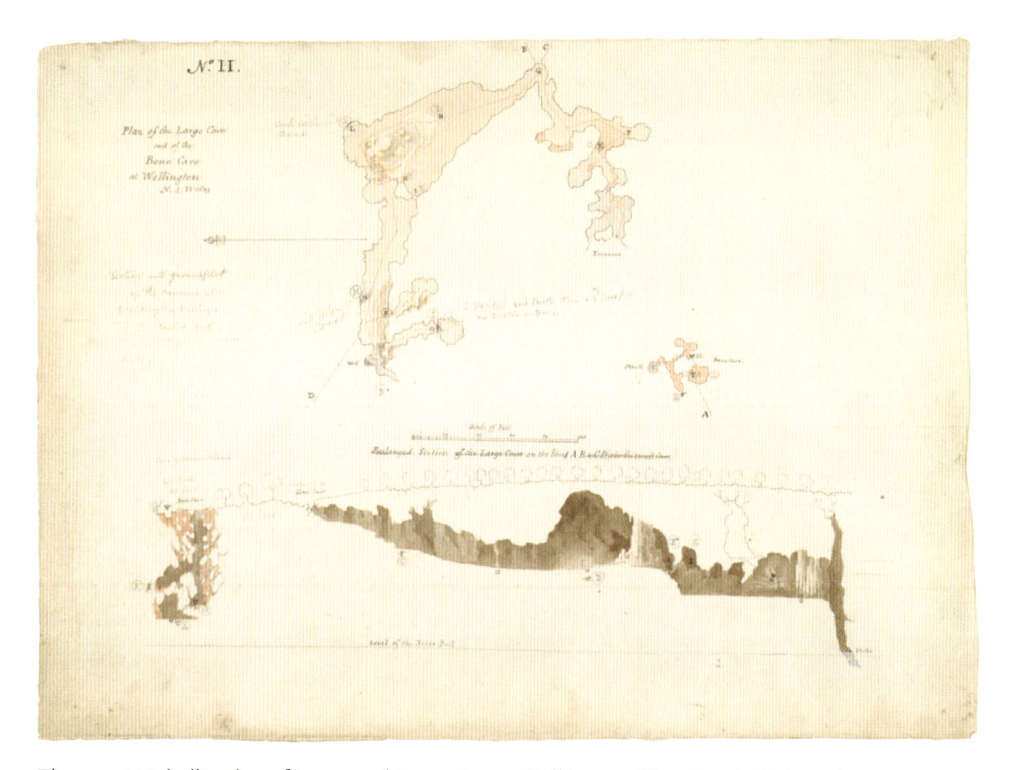

Thomas Mitchell's plan of Large and Bone Caves, Wellington, New South Wales, 1830.

When Mitchell's fossils arrived, however, Owen sought a second opinion from the renowned French palaeontologist Georges Cuvier. Cuvier was one of the first scientists to describe the extinct megafauna of Europe. He realised that the bones of these giant creatures did not belong to any living species, but were from quite different and now extinct animals. Cuvier believed this was evidence of a series of epochs on Earth which had each ended in catastrophic extinctions, perhaps like the biblical flood. Mitchell's fossils from Australia suggested that these catastrophic extinctions had indeed occurred worldwide.

Large Cavern at Wellington Valley, New South Wales, 1839.

Fossils from Wellington Caves may have been part of a worldwide extinction, but they were radically different from any animals found in Europe, past or present. Australia had not been home to (as Cuvier and Owen might have hoped) giant elephants and big cats, but giant marsupials. This finding gave great strength to the evolutionary arguments of Charles Darwin who argued that the modern species had evolved from different ancient species.

Naracoorte Caves

The finds in the Wellington Caves sparked similar interest in cave deposits in other parts of Australia. In 1859 Reverend Tenison-Woods found large fossil bones in the limestone caves near Naracoorte in southern South Australia, close to the Victorian border. He believed, like Cuvier, that these extinct giants provided evidence of a biblical flood.

Although the caves became a popular tourist attraction, it was not until 1908 that any further serious searching for fossils was conducted there. Edward Stirling, a surgeon and physiologist at Adelaide University, excavated teeth of the marsupial lion *Thylacoleo carnifex*. Stirling went on to find important fossils at Lake Callabonna in central South Australia, and helped reconstruct a fossil *Diprotodon* for the South Australian Museum.

Finally, in 1969, enthusiastic members of the Cave Exploration Group of South Australia, Grant Gartrell and Rod Wells, discovered what is now known as the Fossil Chamber in Victoria Cave. Another fossil cave, known as the Ossuaries, was found in the 1970s. The Naracoorte Cave complex has one of the most diverse collections of Pleistocene fossils in Australia and is home to the Wonambi Fossil Centre, providing an opportunity for visitors to experience life in Pleistocene southern Australia.

Western Australian caves

Until recently many of the Pleistocene megafauna were known only from fragments of bone—a jaw here and a vertebra there. But in 2002 that all changed when cavers on the Nullarbor Plains dropped into an underground cave containing complete, untouched skeletons of over thirty different species, including *Thylacoleo* and giant kangaroos. These caves are arguably one of the most significant Pleistocene sites in Australia. Complete skeletons provide vital information about extinct species that can rarely be gleaned from fragments alone. In recognition of their significance, the caves were named the Thylacoleo Caves.

Fossil bones on the floor of the Thylacoleo Caves in Western Australia (jawbones of *Procoptodon goliah* in view).

The Thylacoleo Caves have dramatically improved our understanding of many Pleistocene species, as well as the nature of the environment they lived in. While the climate of the Nullarbor in the Pleistocene was probably dry and arid as it is today, it may not have been as treeless as its name (*nulla arbor* or 'no tree') suggests. Deep beneath the surface are the traces of a time when the Nullarbor was covered in a rich mosaic of shrubs and woodlands, very different from the spinifex grassland of today. Among the eight new species discovered, two were clearly tree-kangaroos, whose modern relatives are entirely adapted to life in the trees.

Other Western Australian caves have also revealed important Pleistocene finds, particularly the Mammoth and Tight Entrance Caves of the Margaret River region.

Lake and river deposits

Just as caves form natural traps or collection points for fossil remains, water provides another ideal environment for trapping and then preserving animals. Kings Creek on the Darling Downs of south-eastern Queensland for example, has accumulated, covered and then exposed a diverse array of bone fragments of late Pleistocene species, many of which are found nowhere else. Other sites, like the dry lakebeds of inland Australia, are fragile and transient, vulnerable to the vagaries of wind and weather to expose and destroy their fossil features.

Early research by Edward Stirling on fossils exposed by erosion on the floor of Lake Callabonna in South Australia documented some of the earliest entire skeletons of *Diprotodons*. Some of the skeletons have since disappeared as the elements have taken their toll. In Victoria, the shallow lakes of the Western District and northern regions conceal megafaunal trackways which are only exposed in times of extreme drought. Cuddie Springs in northern New South Wales has been the site of major excavations since 1933 and has yielded important information about when the megafauna went extinct and whether they co-existed with humans.

Swamps too, can hide their treasures beneath well-disguised surfaces, and bringing them to light can be very difficult, as researchers found at Lancefield in Victoria. Giant bones were first found here in 1843. James Mayne was digging a well in a swampy area just south-west of the town when he uncovered a number of large bones, including a *Diprotodon* jaw. Water prevented further large-scale exploration of the deposit until the 1970s, when pumps could be used to remove water from the excavated sites. Scientists found a thick layer of thousands of

Kangaroo tracks from the Pleistocene, Western District, Victoria.

bones of giant kangaroos, carnivorous *Thylacoleos*, *Diprotodons* and the giant flightless birds *Genyornis newtoni*.

The Lancefield deposit might have been relatively recent, with charcoal from the site dating to around 30 000 years ago. The Lancefield megafauna probably died out between 50 000 and 40 000 years ago, well after the arrival of people in the area. Lancefield, just north of Melbourne, is not far from the extinct Mount William volcano, a significant source of greenstone for local tribes. The co-existence of humans and megafauna is demonstrated at Lancefield by the presence of two stone artefacts among the bones.

What do the fossils reveal?

Pleistocene fossils occur across mainland Australia, as well as in Tasmania and New Guinea. There are also examples of Aboriginal rock art that may depict megafauna. The distribution of these sites provides important clues about where these species lived and the habitats they lived in.

Just because a species lived in an area does not mean that there will be fossils in that area. Fossils only form under particular geological conditions, such as in caves, swamps or rivers. There have been many more fossil finds in the southern and eastern parts of Australia than the north and west, perhaps because of the different climatic and geological conditions, or perhaps because there are fewer people in that area to look for fossils. Thus, fossil locations only provide a general idea of where species lived.

To determine where extinct species may have lived, we need to look at where similar modern species are found and where particular habitats and rainfall areas were in the Pleistocene. Many species tend to cluster in biogeographic zones, which can be defined as the 'northern', 'southern', 'south-eastern', 'south-western', 'eastern' and 'inland' zones. These patterns have been used in this book to estimate what the range of each species might have been.

Fossils can also reveal the size, physiology, eating habits and behaviour of many species. Species with flat grinding teeth often eat plants, while sharp incisors or canine teeth and shearing carnassials often indicate a carnivorous diet. Animal behaviour is, however, notoriously flexible, and sometimes an animal's bones and biology give little indication of how it lives. Modern molecular research, however, has the potential to reveal far more precise information about what an animal actually ate and the environment it lived in.

PREHISTORIC GIANTS: THE MEGAFAUNA OF AUSTRALIA

Many species are known only from a fragment of jaw or a piece of foot bone so we do not always have the luxury of an entire skeleton for each species. Estimating the overall size and weight of a particular individual (let alone the average size of the species) from such fragmentary evidence is extraordinarily difficult. Thus, the estimates of size and weight offered in this book are merely the current best estimates of scientists to date, based on the available evidence.

But no matter how scarce the evidence, or how much scientists debate how big or how fierce one animal is compared to another, the Pleistocene megafauna remain a fascinating part of Australia's recent past. Once upon a time, Aboriginal Australians may have hunted alongside *Thylacoleos* and giant reptiles. They could have co-existed with wombats and *Diprotodons* the size of small cars, they tracked the footprints of 'geese' bigger than emus and they feasted on a suite of kangaroos unlike any we see today. And they painted what appear to be images of many of these creatures on the rock walls of caves and shelters. There have been a great many weird and wonderful beasts on Earth in the past, but the megafauna were so close—they seem to have existed within human history—and it is this relative proximity that makes the lives and demise of these great beasts so fascinating.

In the next few chapters we will meet each of the megafaunal groups and discover what they looked like, what they ate, and where and how they lived, based on the fossil evidence found so far.

Rock painting of Thylacine in Arnhem Land

The megafauna

Marsupial meat-eaters

Australia has relatively few large animals. Despite its size, Australia's poor soils seem unable to support the large numbers of large animals seen on other continents. Australia has never had great herds of wildebeest, bison or buffalo and it has probably never had many large carnivores to prey upon them. In the Pleistocene, as today, carnivores were relatively rare, but they made up for their scarcity by being strikingly unusual.

On other continents most meat-eaters belong to the order Carnivora, a specialist clan of hunters comprising the cats, dogs, bears, raccoons, weasels, civets and hyenas. But in Australia the top predators came from very different backgrounds. The reptilian predators such as the giant crocodiles were perhaps not too surprising, but from the ranks of the seemingly gentle marsupials came some startlingly ferocious Pleistocene killers.

Thylacinus cyanocephalus

PREHISTORIC GIANTS: THE MEGAFAUNA OF AUSTRALIA

Thylacoleo

CLASS: Mammalia
SUPERCOHORT: Marsupialia
ORDER: Diprotodontia
FAMILY: Thylacoleonidae

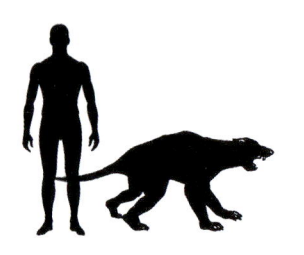

EXTINCT SPECIES		LENGTH	WEIGHT
Thylacoleo	*Thylacoleo carnifex*	1.90 m	130 kg
LIVING COMPARISON			
Jaguar	*Panthera onca*	1.85 m	130 kg

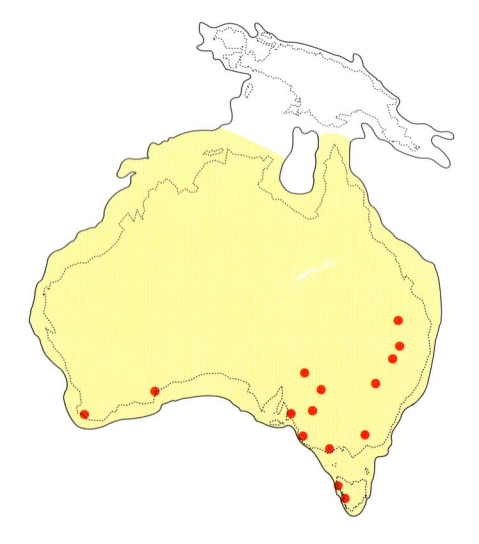

Fossil sites and possible distribution of *Thylacoleo*

Thylacoleo carnifex—the Marsupial Lion—probably behaved a bit like a modern leopard or jaguar. Yet surprisingly, its closest relatives were the diprotodons and wombats that may have formed the bulk of its prey.

Thylacoleo's teeth were clearly adapted for eating meat. When Richard Owen first described it in 1859, he named it the butchering (*carnifex*) marsupial lion (*Thylacoleo*). He thought it was 'the fellest of all predatory beasts'. Not everyone agreed—Gerard Krefft, director of the Australian Museum, insisted *Thylacoleo* was a herbivore. He thought its great shearing teeth were for eating melons. But modern analysis confirms that the long sharp incisors and slicing premolars are clearly adaptations for hunting and eating meat. *Thylacoleo's* short strong jaw also gave it a massively strong bite, typical of animals that hunt creatures bigger than themselves.

Thylacoleo was undoubtedly a proficient and well-equipped hunter

    Thylacoleo might have killed small prey by biting their necks and strangled larger prey by biting their trachea, just as African lions hunt today. *Thylacoleo's* semi-opposable thumb, with its long, hooked claw in a retractable sheath, would have given it a frightening grip on its prey.

    Thylacoleo seems to have lived mainly in the open forest and margins, although it has also been found in the Nullarbor, which at the time was covered with low, shrubby woodland. We can tell from its skeleton that *Thylacoleo* was a running animal, quite agile and probably good at climbing trees. Like most mammalian predators, it probably hunted at night or in the early hours of dawn and dusk.

PREHISTORIC GIANTS: THE MEGAFAUNA OF AUSTRALIA

Skull (left) and skeleton (right) of *Thylacoleo* from the Nullabor Caves

We cannot tell from fossils how *Thylacoleo* raised its young, but most active marsupials soon leave their growing young in a den or nest while they hunt or forage. Large predators typically only have two or three young per litter, as it often takes a long time for young predators to learn the skills they need to survive.

Thylacine

CLASS: Mammalia
SUPERCOHORT: Marsupialia
ORDER: Dasyuromorphia
FAMILY: Thylacinidae

EXTINCT SPECIES		LENGTH	WEIGHT
Thylacine	*Thylacinus cyanocephalus*	1.75 m	35 kg
LIVING COMPARISON			
Dingo	*Canis lupus dingo*	1.20 m	24 kg

Strictly speaking, the Thylacine, or Tasmanian Tiger, is not one of the 'megafauna', although some of its predecessors from the late Miocene were certainly giants (such as *Thylacinus potens* from Alcoota, north-east of Alice Springs). But the Thylacine we know weighed less than forty-five kilograms and, more importantly, it survived into the modern era—at least until recently. Thylacines were still present in Tasmania when Europeans first settled there and found the colonists free-ranging sheep herds irresistible. With a bounty on their pelts, Thylacines were rapidly exterminated. Within eighty years, Thylacines were rare in Tasmania and the last known individual died in captivity in 1936. Some people believe that Thylacines might still survive in the wilderness of western Tasmania, but there have been no confirmed sightings.

The extinction of the Thylacine was not just due to Europeans however. The species was once widespread across Australia. Rock art images of the marsupial 'tigers' with their distinctive stripes occur as far north as Kakadu. But during the Pleistocene the Thylacine's range shrank, perhaps as a result of climate change or competition with the Dingo, which arrived in Australia about four thousand years ago. By the end of the Pleistocene Thylacines lived only in the far south and were soon isolated in Tasmania by the rising sea levels of Bass Strait.

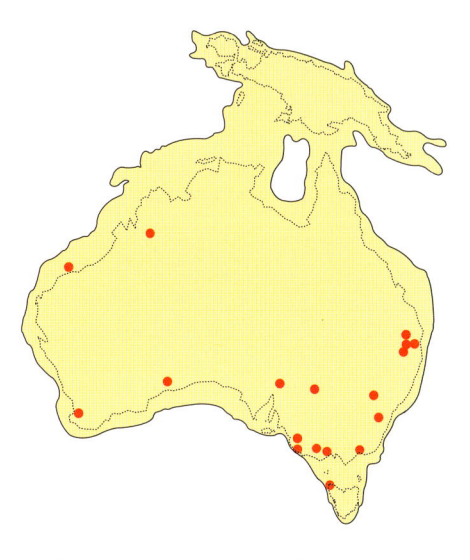

Australia's largest surviving carnivorous mammal, the Tasmanian Devil (*Sarcophilus laniarius*), was also present in the Pleistocene. Like many species, Pleistocene devils were larger than their modern counterparts (which weigh up to eight kilograms), but at just eighteen kilograms (not even as big as a Dingo) they can hardly be regarded as giants.

Fossil sites and possible distribution of Thylacine

The last-known live Thylacine died in captivity in 1936 at Beaumaris Zoo, Hobart.

PREHISTORIC GIANTS: THE MEGAFAUNA OF AUSTRALIA

Giant Rat-kangaroo

CLASS: Mammalia
SUPERCOHORT: Marsupialia
ORDER: Diprotodontia
SUPERFAMILY: Macropodoidea
FAMILY: Potoroidae
SUBFAMILY: Propleopinae

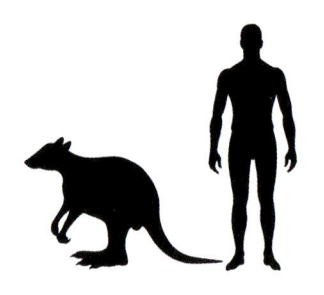

EXTINCT SPECIES		LENGTH	WEIGHT
Giant Rat-kangaroo	*Propleopus oscillans*	2.00 m	45–60 kg
	Propleopus chillagoensis		
	Propleopus wellingtonensis		
LIVING COMPARISON			
Common Wallaroo	*Macropus robustus*	1.99 m	46 kg

For eighty years the Giant Rat-kangaroo *Propleopus oscillans* was known only from a lower jawbone found on the Darling Downs in south-eastern Queensland. But even this small fragment told us that this creature was something unusual. The jaw most closely resembled that of the living Musky Rat-kangaroo (*Hypsiprymnodon moschatus*), a small, secretive creature living in the rainforests of northern Queensland. But while the Musky Rat-kangaroo weighs barely more than half a kilogram, this jawbone came from an animal that may have weighed as much as sixty kilograms—the size of a modern Red Kangaroo.

In the last fifty years a small number of fragmentary remains of *Propleopus* have been found across south-eastern Australia. Most of these are teeth and jaws, although an upper arm bone has been found. But even these fragments reveal a startling change in lifestyle. Rat-kangaroos are generally omnivores; some specialising in forest fungi, while others eat insects and plants. Modern rat-kangaroos will occasionally scavenge animal carcasses, but this is generally rare. *Propleopus*, however, seems to have taken these omnivorous tendencies even further. Its strongly serrated premolars are for slicing and holding tough material such as meat, and the ridges along the base of the molars seem to prevent bone splinters from piercing the gums. But the most persuasive evidence of all that *Propleopus* was a meat-eater comes from the microscopic wear patterns on its premolars, which shows grooving characteristic of carnivores, but not herbivores.

Modern finds suggest that three *Propleopus* species occurred in the Pleistocene. *Propleopus oscillans*, the first species to be described, seems to have retained the grinding molars of a herbivore in addition to its carnivorous shearing teeth. Many modern carnivores (like foxes) include a large amount of plant material in their diet, and many species commonly regarded as herbivores (including rat-kangaroos and some primates) become effective hunters when the opportunity arises. *Propleopus oscillans* seems to have been similarly adaptable in its food preferences.

The more northern *Propleopus chillagoensis*, from the Chillagoe Caves in north-eastern Queensland, however, seems to have been a more dedicated carnivore. Its rear molars are much smaller, more like those of *Thylacoleo* or modern carnivores. Other fossil species found at the same site suggest that it lived in a dense woodland environment, unlike its southern cousin *Propleopus oscillans*, which ranged from the open forests of the east into the colder, arid, treeless environments of southern Victoria and the inland.

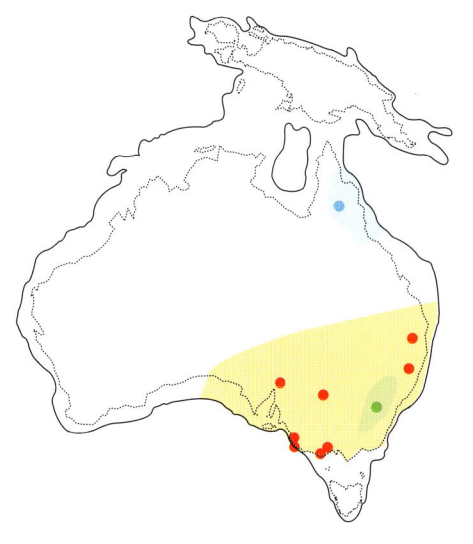

Fossil sites and possible distribution of

● ▢ *Propleopus oscillans*
● ▓ *Propleopus wellingtonensis*
● ▓ *Propleopus chillagoensis*

Little is known of the third species, *Propleopus wellingtonensis*, from the Bone Cave deposits of the Wellington Caves in New South Wales, but the teeth found are significantly longer than any of those for *Propleopus oscillans*, suggesting that it was certainly a different species and may have been even larger.

Cold-blooded killers

Mammals are not the only predators in Australia. In fact, our largest modern carnivore is not a mammal at all, but a reptile. Residents of northern Australia (and some unlucky tourists) know just how dangerous predators like crocodiles can be. In the Pleistocene, there were even more species of giant predatory reptiles. Imagine what Australia would have been like when giant goannas and crocodiles stalked the continent?

Megalania prisca

Giant Goanna

CLASS: Reptilia
SUBCLASS: Lepidosauria
ORDER: Squamata
FAMILY: Varanidae

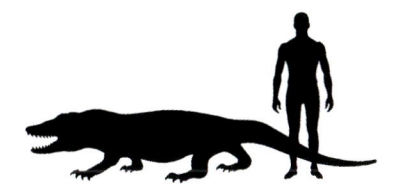

EXTINCT SPECIES		LENGTH	WEIGHT
Giant Goanna	*Megalania prisca*	5.70 m	1000 kg
LIVING COMPARISON			
Komodo Dragon	*Varanus komodoensis*	3.00 m	60 kg

Exactly how big the Giant Goanna (*Megalania prisca*, also known as *Varanus priscus*) grew is a matter of great debate. Early calculations based on a single foot bone suggested that the animal might have grown up to seven metres in length and weighed over half a tonne. The maximum sizes of megafauna tend to be a bit like 'the fish that got away'—they get bigger and bigger with retelling. Some accounts describe *Megalania* as being as big as an allosaurus, weighing several tonnes. Very conservative estimates suggest a maximum of just five metres and a weight of one-hundred and forty kilograms—not quite twice the size of the modern Komodo Dragon. Based on the few fossils we have, it seems most likely that *Megalania* grew to similar sizes to the modern Saltwater Crocodile.

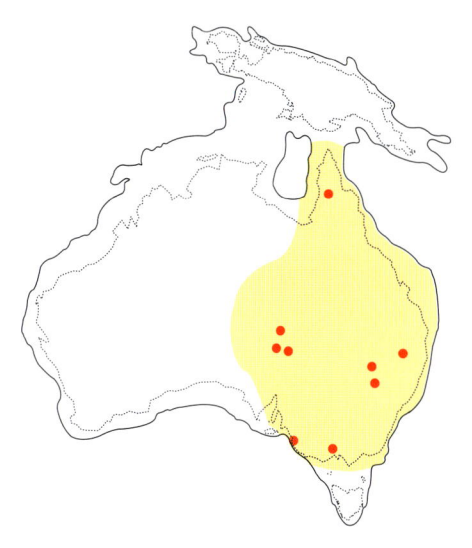

Fossil sites and possible distribution of *Megalania*

Megalania fossils are quite rare. A partial skeleton and other isolated fragments were found at Kings Creek in the Darling Downs in the nineteenth century.

A skeletal reconstruction of *Megalania* at Museum Victoria

The most complete specimen was found in 1965 in eastern Queensland when French geologists brought three large vertebrae into the Queensland Museum. Museum staff returned to the site, uncovering a few ribs, teeth and part of a jaw. But their activities inspired the interest of the son of the land manager. After the palaeontologists had left, the twelve-year-old continued his own excavations. He uncovered still more ribs, part of a pelvis and jaw, a leg bone and numerous other small fragments. Thirty years later, Mr Hawkins, now a geologist himself, donated the material to the Queensland Museum where it makes up the most complete known skeleton of a *Megalania*.

Megalania was probably an ambush predator, only running short distances to bring down its prey. Being cold-blooded, it would not have required as much food as a large mammalian carnivore and its large size would have helped even out the fluctuations in temperature that trouble smaller reptiles.

Most large modern monitors shelter in a den or burrow of some kind and, despite its large size, it seems likely that *Megalania* would have done this also, either using caves or undergrowth or digging its own. They may even have taken over wombat burrows. One *Megalania* specimen had a single acid-etched wombat tooth lying among its ribs.

Because few fossils of *Megalania* have been found, we know relatively little about how it would have lived. A few tantalising skull fragments reveal a crest, leading some scientists to suggest that male *Megalania* may have fought with each other using their heads like wrecker's balls. The fact that several of the few ribs found have old healed fractures lend weight to this theory, and at least reveal that life was not always easy for this top-level predator.

Crocodiles

CLASS: Reptilia
SUBCLASS: Sauropsida
ORDER: Crocodilia
FAMILY: Crocodylidae
SUBFAMILY: Mekosuchinae

EXTINCT SPECIES		LENGTH	WEIGHT
Giant Crocodile	*Pallimnarchus pollens*	5.50 m	1000 kg
Land Crocodile	*Quinkana fortirostrum*	3.00 m	120 kg
LIVING COMPARISON			
Saltwater Crocodile	*Crocodylus porosus*	5.50 m	1000 kg

Giant crocodiles were once common across the world and were much more diverse than they are today. In the Cretaceous, an American giant *Deinosuchus*

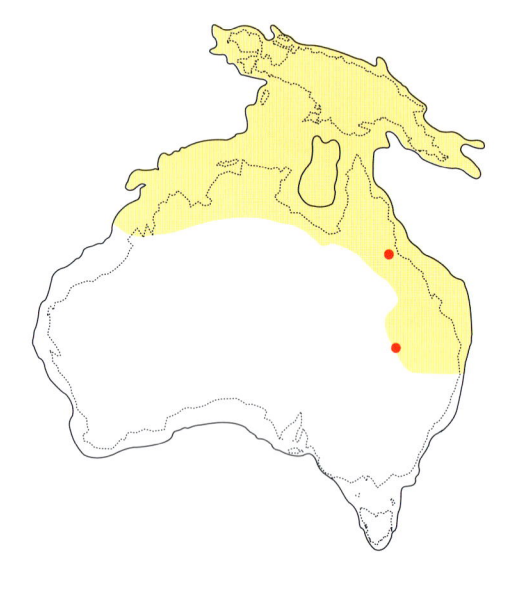

Fossil sites and possible distribution of *Pallimnarchus pollens* and *Quinkana fortirostrum*

may have grown up to ten metres and weighed up to five tonnes. At the same time, the African lakes were terrorised by *Sarcosuchus imperator*, which apparently grew up to twelve metres long and weighed eight tonnes.

Some of these giants were ziphodonts, an ancient type of land crocodile with wide, high snouts and teeth serrated like steak-knives. Widespread around the world, they had largely died out by the Miocene (when many modern mammalian carnivores emerged) but they survived longer in Australia, right into the Pleistocene and the age of humans.

A ziphodont skull, with its characteristic broad, deep snout, was first found by a caver in Tea Tree Cave near Chillagoe in northern Queensland in 1970. Scientists named this crocodile *Quinkana* after the quinkan, mythical creatures from the Dreamtime. Further discoveries have revealed that it was a member of a diverse group of ziphodont crocodiles found in northern Australia. *Quinkana fortirostrum* was the last of these land crocodiles. Its rounded (rather than flattened) tail and hoof-like claws suggest a terrestrial rather than aquatic lifestyle. The Pleistocene *Quinkana* was not as big as some of its earlier forebears, but it still grew to more than three metres in length.

Fearsome though *Quinkana fortirostrum* must have been, it was probably dwarfed by the mighty *Pallimnarchus pollens*. This broad-snouted crocodile occupied inland waters in northern Australia and was probably about the same size as the modern Salt-water Crocodile. Very little else is known about it, as there are only a handful of fossil remains, the largest of which is a nearly complete skull from near Townsville in northern Queensland.

Although *Quinkana* may have been more terrestrial than other crocodiles, it still seems likely that both *Pallimnarchus* and *Quinkana* would have been found around the waterways of the northern coasts. Both species probably buried their eggs in nests, using the surrounding temperature to hatch them. These giant predators would certainly have terrorised any animals coming to drink at waterholes, as evidenced by quinkan teeth marks found in fossil emu bones. But they may also have been (like modern crocodiles) gentle protective parents, digging up their young as they hatched and carrying them to safety.

The crocodiles also offer us a rare survivor of the Pleistocene megafauna. The Saltwater Crocodile (*Crocodylus porosus*) shared the northern Australian coastline with these extinct cousins, along with the smaller Australian Freshwater Crocodile (*Crocodylus johnstoni*). Imagine what life must have been like when not one, but three, species of giant crocodiles lurked around our northern waterways.

The modern saltwater crocodile reveals what the extinct giant may have been like

Snakes

CLASS: Reptilia
SUBCLASS: Lepidosauria
ORDER: Squamata
FAMILY: Boidae
SUBFAMILY: Madtsoiinae

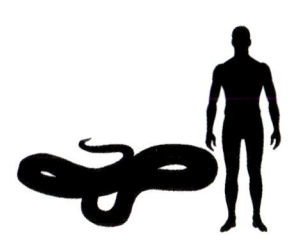

31

PREHISTORIC GIANTS: THE MEGAFAUNA OF AUSTRALIA

EXTINCT SPECIES		LENGTH	WEIGHT
Giant Python	*Wonambi naracoortensis*	5.00 m	50 kg
LIVING COMPARISON			
Amethystine Python	*Morelia kinghorni*	5.50 m	70 kg

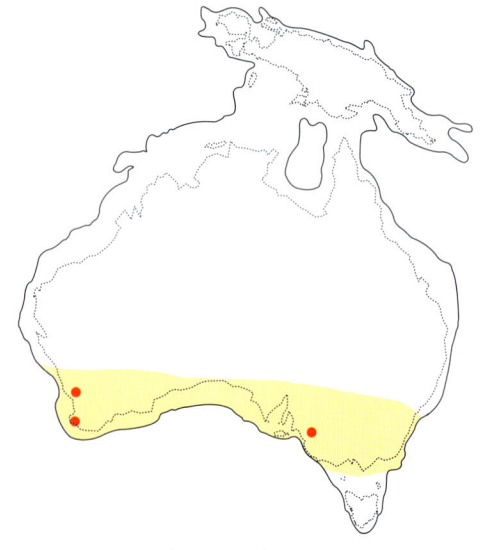

Fossil sites and possible distribution of *Wonambi*

The giant python *Wonambi naracoortensis* was named for the great rainbow serpent of the Pitjantjatjara Dreaming. *Wonambi* probably belongs to an ancient family of madtsoiidae snakes, which were once abundant across Gondwana. They may have been the largest snakes that ever existed—one African relative *Gigantophis garstini* may have grown to nine metres long. While madtsoiid snakes died out on all other continents more than fifty-five million years ago, they continued to thrive in Australia until the Pleistocene, just fifty thousand years ago. *Wonambi naracoortensis* was the last surviving member of its subfamily.

Despite its large size *Wonambi* had a relatively small head, so perhaps it ate only small or medium size prey. It would have captured its prey in much the same way as large pythons do today, coiling its body around its victim and slowly suffocating it. Most large snakes of this size today are aquatic and live in tropical areas where the warm environment keeps them active. Yet *Wonambi* lived in the Naracoorte Caves area where the winters were cool, much like today. Cold weather may well have kept this large snake inactive for much of the year and may have meant it grew and reproduced only slowly. If it was a cave-dweller it may have fed on the abundant bats that roosted, and still roost, in the Naracoorte Caves today.

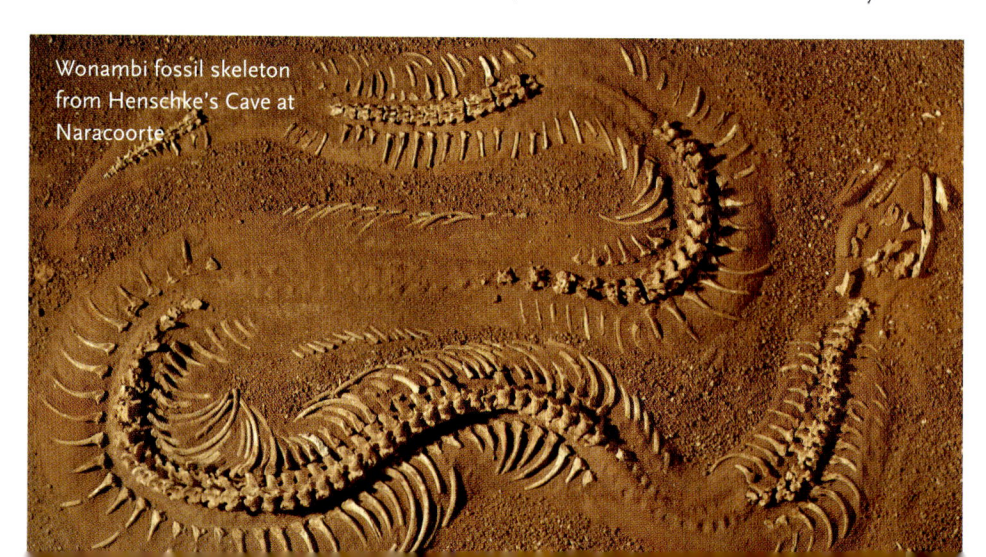

Wonambi fossil skeleton from Henschke's Cave at Naracoorte

Tortoises

CLASS: Reptilia
SUBCLASS: Sauropsida
ORDER: Testudines
FAMILY: Meiolaniidae

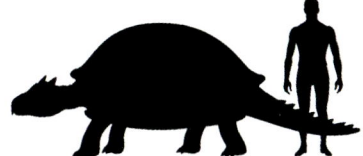

EXTINCT SPECIES		LENGTH	WEIGHT
Lord Howe Horned Tortoise	*Meiolania platyceps*	2.00 m	500 kg
Ninja Tortoise	*Ninjemys oweni*	3.00 m	750 kg
LIVING COMPARISON			
Galapagos Giant Tortoise	*Geochelone nigra*	1.20 m	300 kg

Not all of the Pleistocene reptiles were cold-blooded killers, although the enormous horned tortoises certainly would have looked fearsome enough. Their large knobbly heads with long horns, and their heavily armoured and spiked tail, belied their herbivorous nature. The meiolanids were land tortoises with stumpy, clawed feet and probably behaved much like the Galapagos Giant Tortoise—except that they were twice as big.

Horned tortoises laid large clutches of eggs, just like modern tortoises do. Despite their heavy armour, they probably grazed peacefully on grasses and shrubs. Like most large modern turtles they were likely to have been long-lived, with lifespans of up to two hundred years.

Fossils of horned tortoises occur across northern Australia and on Pacific islands such as New Caledonia and Lord Howe Island. The last surviving

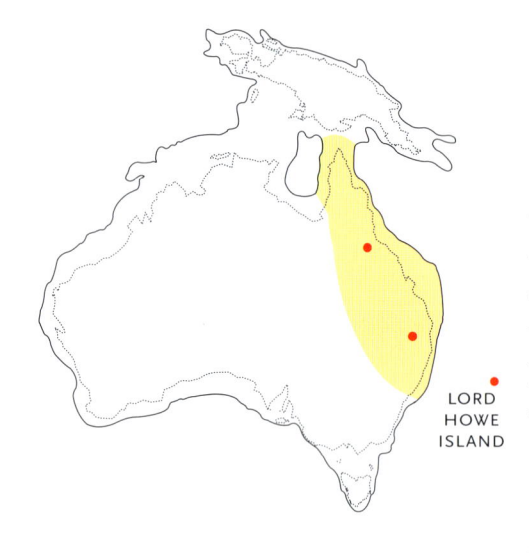

Fossil sites and possible distribution of *Meiolania*

Lord Howe Island, off the coast of New South Wales, provides some of the best preserved complete specimens of horned tortoises.

species lived in New Caledonia as recently as 2000 years ago. The best-preserved and most abundant fossils of *Meiolania platyceps* are from Lord Howe Island, but similar fossils also occur across central and northern Australia. These animals were about two metres long and, based on the smaller Galapagos tortoises, may have weighed half a tonne. Fragments of a very similar species have been found at Wyandotte Station in northern Queensland. The horns of this species are twice the size of those of the Lord Howe Island species, so either it had much bigger horns or it was a much bigger animal.

The skull and tail bones of another large tortoise, *Meiolania oweni*, have been found in Darling Downs in Central Queensland. This tortoise had backward-pointing horns and a large, bony neck frill. It was at least one and half times bigger than the Lord Howe Horned Tortoise, making it considerably heavier than even the largest Saltwater Crocodile. Some scientists believe this tortoise belongs to a different genus, dubbing it *Ninjemys oweni*, or the Ninja Turtle.

With their formidable size and armoury, it is hard to imagine what might have threatened the horned tortoises, and why they went extinct. Like the Galapagos tortoises, which comprise many small populations of subspecies on different islands, the horned tortoises of the Pleistocene were isolated fragments of a formerly widespread family that once ranged across Gondwana. Small isolated populations are highly vulnerable to extinction through chance events—climate and sea level change, introduced competition, predation or disease— and long-lived, slow-breeding species like turtles are particularly vulnerable to such environmental change.

Genyornis newtoni

The big birds

There were many 'upsized' Australian birds in the Pleistocene although few attained the size of the flightless moas of New Zealand or the Elephant Bird of Madagascar. Raptors once spread their wings even wider than modern wedge-tailed eagles and great flocks of pink flamingos prattled around Australian waterholes. But, as the climate grew drier and the vast inland lakes disappeared, most of these species vanished from our shores.

PREHISTORIC GIANTS: THE MEGAFAUNA OF AUSTRALIA

Mihirung

CLASS: Aves
ORDER: Anseriformes
FAMILY: Dromornithidae

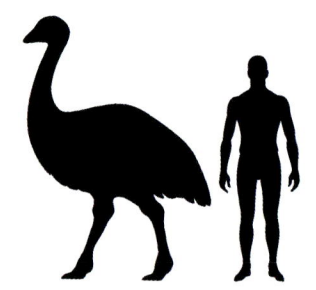

EXTINCT SPECIES		HEIGHT	WEIGHT
Newton's Mihirung	*Genyornis newtoni*	2.15 m	275 kg
LIVING COMPARISON			
Emu	*Dromaius novaehollandiae*	2.00 m	45 kg

Modern Australia is home to two of the world's biggest birds—the Cassowary of the northern rainforests and the Emu of the inland plains. But in the Pleistocene, the Emu shared the open woodlands with the much larger and considerably heavier mihirung. The mihirung were the last survivors of a family of uniquely Australian birds that had dominated the landscape for over fifty million years. These giant flightless birds were related to ducks and geese. Around eight different species have been identified, the largest of all being *Dromornis stirtoni* of the late Miocene, which stood three metres tall and weighed over half a tonne.

By the Pleistocene, however, only one mihirung remained. *Genyornis newtoni* was of a medium build for a mihirung, not much taller than a modern Emu but ten times as solid. The first three *Genyornis* skeletons were found embedded in Lake Callabona clay in 1894, having lain there undisturbed since the great birds were trapped in the drying lakebed fifty thousand years ago. Since then, *Genyornis* bones, footprints and eggs (which would have weighed over a kilogram) have been found right across Australia.

Genyornis newtoni was undoubtedly a plant-eater. Many skeletons have small piles of polished stones in their gizzard area, something many plant-eating birds use to grind up their food. A fossilised *Callitris* pinecone was even found near one skeleton at Lake Callabona. Analysis of *Genyornis* eggshells reveals that they ate mostly leafy greens rather than grasses. Perhaps the shrub-browsing mihirung were not suited to the expanding grasslands of the late Pleistocene.

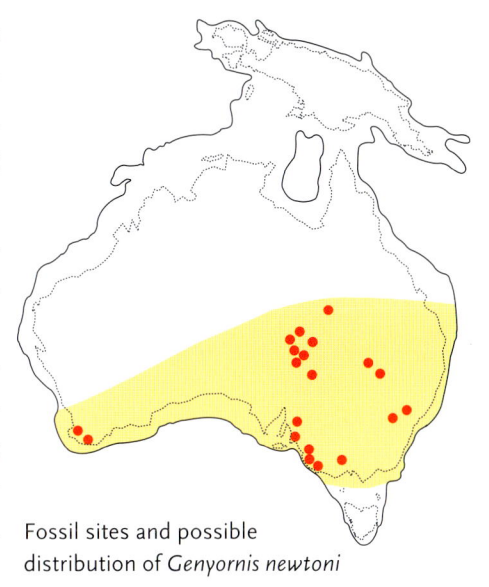

Fossil sites and possible distribution of *Genyornis newtoni*

The large and heavy beak of the earlier mihirung species has led to some speculation that they may have been carnivorous, like the 'terror birds' of South America. However, many birds that eat fruits and leaves, like toucans and hornbills, have large, heavy bills. Ducks and geese generally have big heads for their body size (compared to the small-headed ratites like Emus) and the mihirung seem to follow the same pattern on a bigger scale. They may not have been 'killer ducks' roaming the forests of the Pleistocene but, by their sheer size and weight, a flock of irate mihirung would probably have been worth avoiding.

The mihirung were taller than modern emus and considerably more heavily built

PREHISTORIC GIANTS: THE MEGAFAUNA OF AUSTRALIA

Giant Malleefowl

CLASS: Aves
ORDER: Galliformes
FAMILY: Megapodiidae

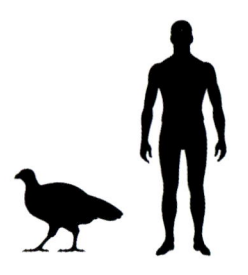

EXTINCT SPECIES		LENGTH	WEIGHT
Giant Malleefowl	*Progura gallinacea*	1.30 m	5–7 kg
LIVING COMPARISON			
Malleefowl	*Leipoa ocellata*	0.60 m	2.5 kg

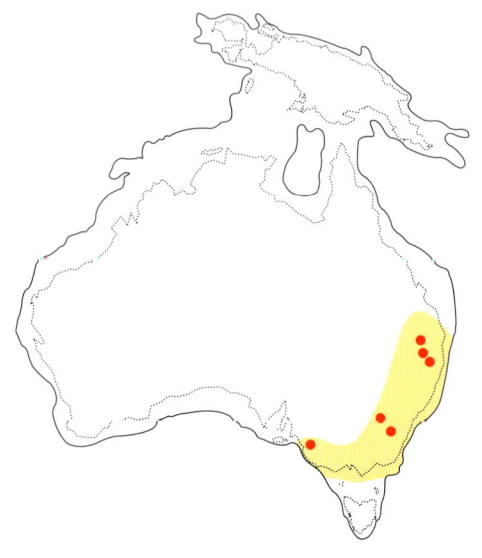

Fossil sites and possible distribution of Giant Malleefowl

Many bird species in the Pleistocene were larger than their modern counterparts, although they did not attain the impressive size of the mihirung. The Giant Malleefowl (*Progura gallinacea*) was probably about the size of a large turkey. It was considerably larger than the modern Malleefowl (*Leipoa ocellata*), which reaches just two and a half kilograms. Malleefowl are members of the megapode family, which lay their eggs in mounds, using the heat from the soil and compost to incubate their eggs. They share this habit with their relatives the scrubfowl and brush-turkeys. Some species even use the heat from rocks in volcanic areas to incubate their eggs.

For a while, scientists thought that there were two species of giant mallee-fowl in southern Australia, one somewhat smaller than the other. Now that more material has been collected, however, scientists think that the two forms are simply the larger males and smaller females of a dimorphic species. Giant megapodes were quite common across the Pacific at this time and included an enormous emu-sized megapode, *Sylviornis neocaledoniae*, in New Caledonia.

Giant Coucal

Class: Aves
Order: Cuculiformes
Family: Cuculidae

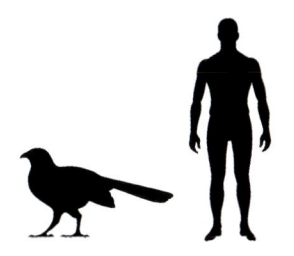

EXTINCT SPECIES		LENGTH	WEIGHT
Giant Coucal	*Centropus colossus*	1.00 m	5.0 kg
LIVING COMPARISON			
Pheasant Coucal	*Centropus phasianinus*	0.80 m	3.8 kg

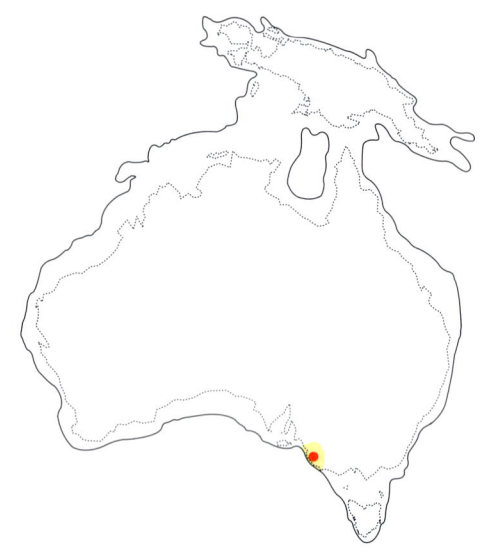

Fossil sites and possible distribution of the Giant Coucal

The Pheasant Coucal of the northern forests of Australia is an appealing, unflappable bird that serenely observes the world from the sheltered secrecy of the thick undergrowth. Named for its mellow booming call, the Pheasant Coucal is the last survivor in Australia of a rainforest genus whose members also include a number of highly endangered species in south-east Asia.

Coucals are part of the oldest bird lineages, and are close relatives of the strange clawed Hoatzin of South America and the parasitic cuckoos. Australia is home to about a dozen different cuckoo species, many of which are characterised, like the coucal, by their smart barred chests and long tails. Nearly all of them are rainforest species with just a few having successfully colonised the arid inland and colder southern regions of Australia.

Unlike the cuckoos, coucals make their own cup-shaped nests and raise their own young. They are ungainly birds, preferring to run along tunnels in the undergrowth rather than fly, although they can do so when disturbed. The Giant Coucal of the Pleistocene was probably even more terrestrial, being a third larger in size and with a smaller attachment area for the chest muscles used in flight. Remains have been found at the Naracoorte Caves, providing further support for the notion that the area may once have been more thickly vegetated than it is today.

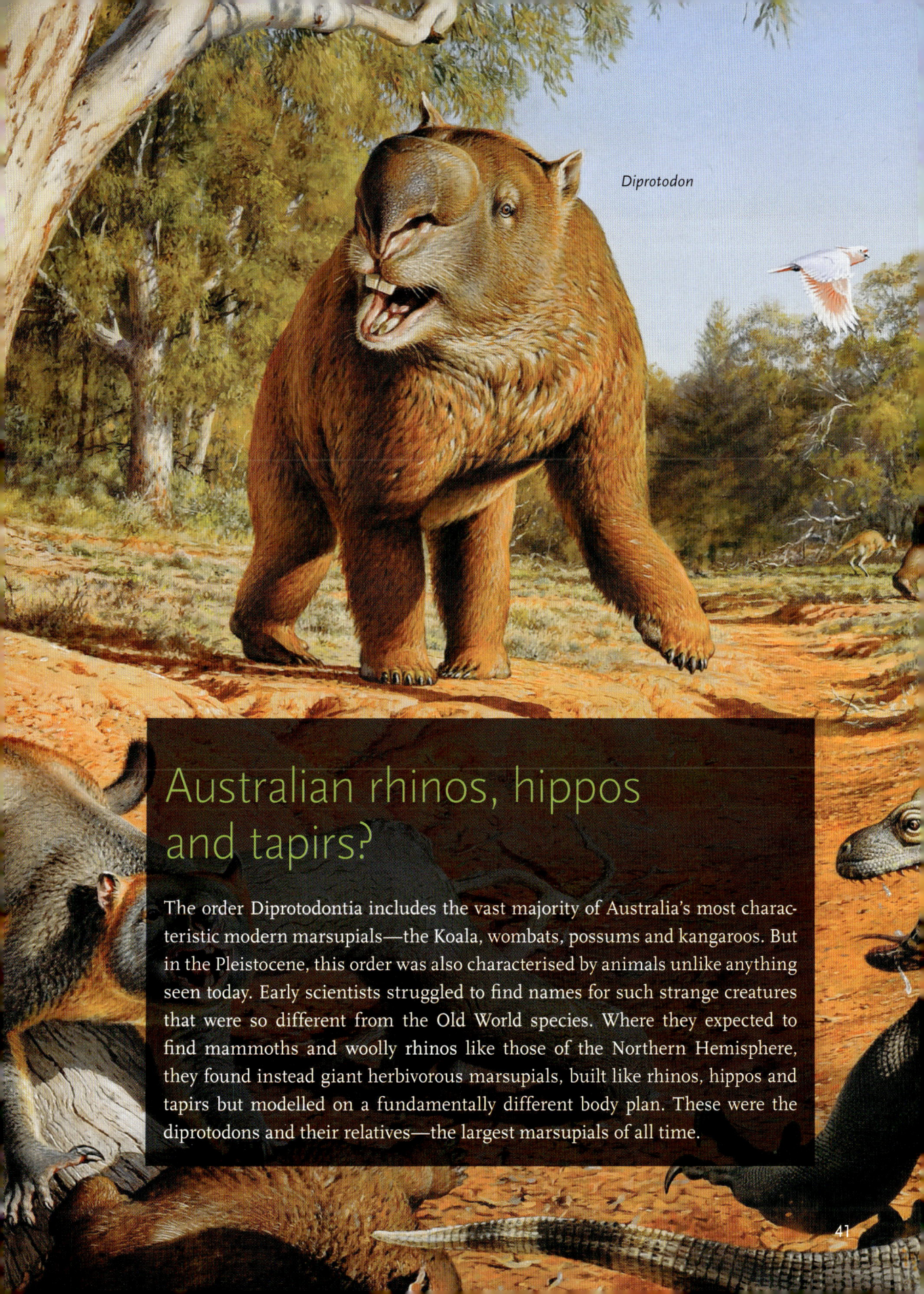

Diprotodon

Australian rhinos, hippos and tapirs?

The order Diprotodontia includes the vast majority of Australia's most characteristic modern marsupials—the Koala, wombats, possums and kangaroos. But in the Pleistocene, this order was also characterised by animals unlike anything seen today. Early scientists struggled to find names for such strange creatures that were so different from the Old World species. Where they expected to find mammoths and woolly rhinos like those of the Northern Hemisphere, they found instead giant herbivorous marsupials, built like rhinos, hippos and tapirs but modelled on a fundamentally different body plan. These were the diprotodons and their relatives—the largest marsupials of all time.

PREHISTORIC GIANTS: THE MEGAFAUNA OF AUSTRALIA

Diprotodons

CLASS: Mammalia
SUPERCOHORT: Marsupialia
ORDER: Diprotodontia
FAMILY: Diprotodontidae

EXTINCT SPECIES		LENGTH	WEIGHT
Giant Diprotodon	*Diprotodon optatum*	3.00 m	2700 kg
	Smaller form (female)	2.30 m	900 kg
LIVING COMPARISON			
White Rhinoceros	*Ceratotherium simum*	3.35 m	2800 kg

The giant *Diprotodon optatum* was the largest of all the Australian megafauna and the largest marsupial ever. Weighing over two tonnes and standing almost two metres high at the shoulder, these solid, heavily built marsupials were the size of a small four-wheel drive. They were the gentle giants of the Pleistocene, browsing on the shrubs and trees of the open woodlands and forests like overgrown wombats.

Diprotodon optatum was widespread across much of Australia but seems to have favoured the inland areas. Smaller specimens were once classified as

Diprotodon minor but are now thought to be smaller females.

The diprotodonts have no close parallel among living animals. The rhinoceros and the hippopotamus of Africa resemble it in size and bulk, but rhinos only graze on grass rather than browsing on bushes, while hippos are not only grazers but are also unusually aquatic. Unlike the heavily armoured rhino and the aggressive hippo, diprotodonts were probably gentle creatures, relying on their sheer bulk for protection from predators. Certainly they seemed to have lived for a long time, as many fossils have the worn down teeth typical of advanced age.

Fossil sites and possible distribution of *Diprotodon optatum*

Diprotodon were unlikely to have fought violently with each other. Complete *Diprotodon* skulls are rarely preserved as fossils because they are unusually thin and fragile, being taken up mainly with large nasal sinuses rather than brains. So however diprotodonts settled their neighbourly disputes, it was not by head-butting each other. Perhaps they signalled their intentions through vocal contests. You can imagine these huge creatures bellowing across the valleys of Pleistocene Australia. Perhaps they just sized each other up, the way many large animals do today,

Articulated cast of a *Diprotodon* at Museum Victoria

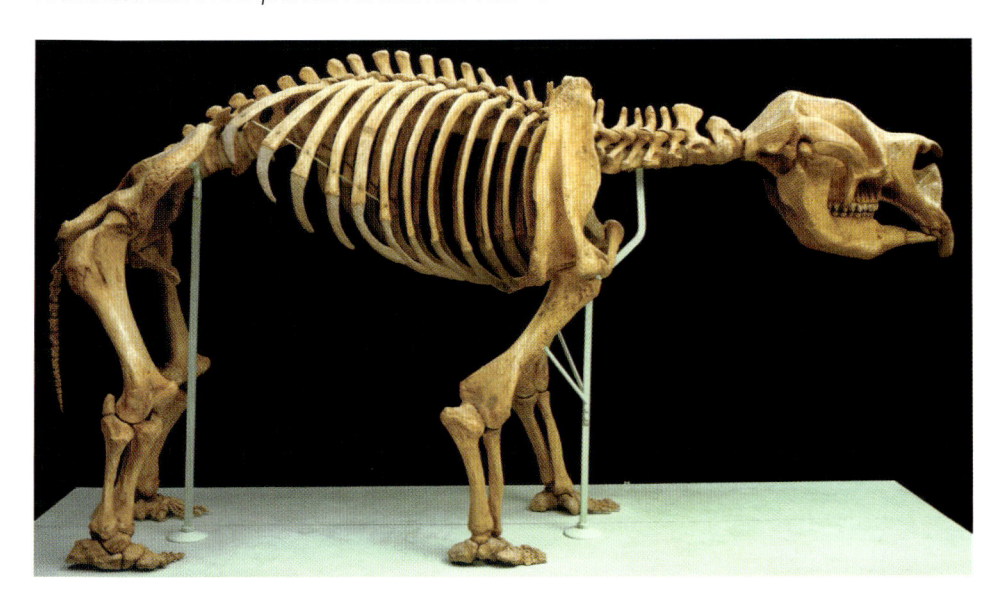

PREHISTORIC GIANTS: THE MEGAFAUNA OF AUSTRALIA

rather than risking an all-out brawl, with the smaller of the pair giving way to the larger after a little bit of 'push me, shove you'.

It is tempting to think of these large animals as heavy lumbering beasts, but they have unusual anatomical features that suggest they may have been more delicate in their movements. Their wrist and ankle bones had rotating ball-and-socket joints, and trackways of their footprints show that they walked on their front toes. Perhaps they used their size to stretch up into the shrubbery to browse, using flexible front feet to manipulate the foliage—which would also explain their need for lighter skulls.

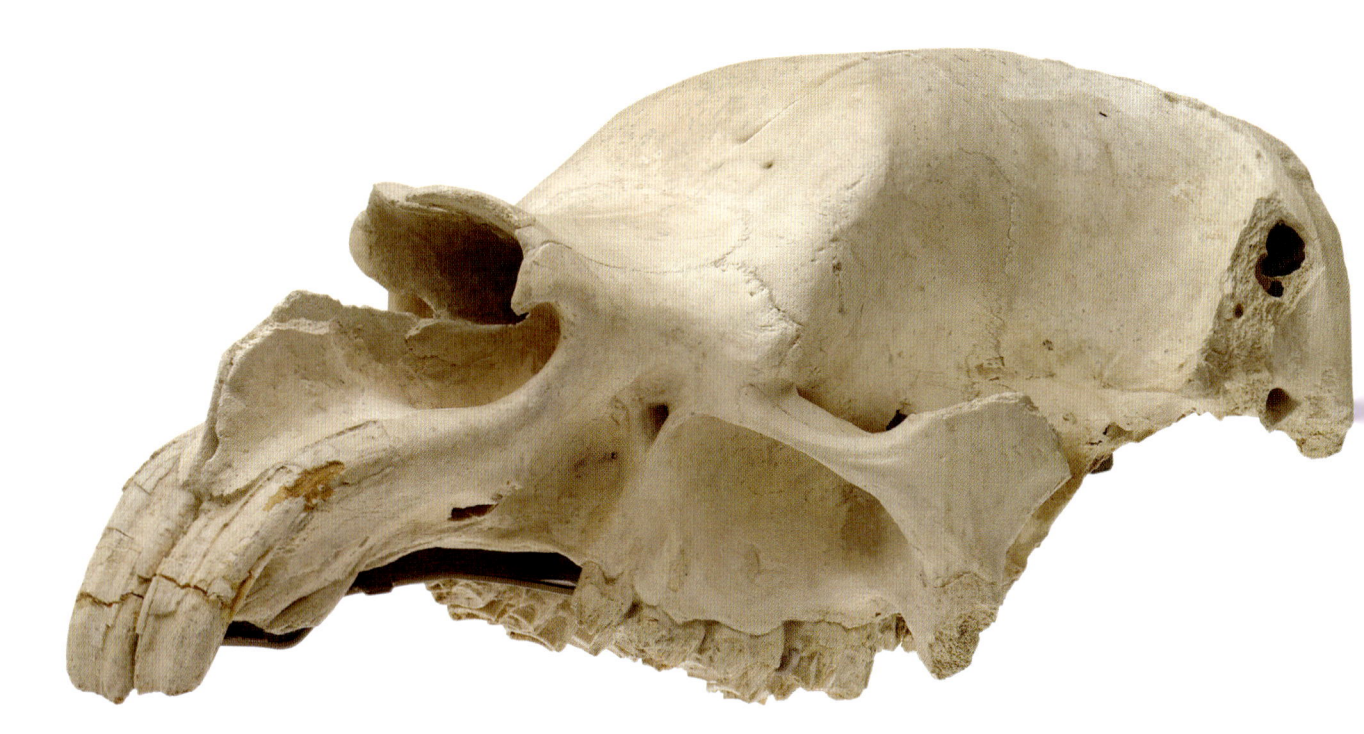

Complete *Diprotodon* skulls are rare, as they are unusually thin and fragile for an animal this size.

Zygomaturus

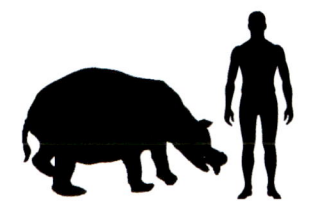

EXTINCT SPECIES		LENGTH	WEIGHT
	Zygomaturus trilobus	2.00 m	500 kg
	Zygomaturus tasmanicus	1.50 m	300 kg
LIVING COMPARISON			
Pygmy hippopotamus	*Hexaprotodon liberiensis*	1.50 m	250 kg

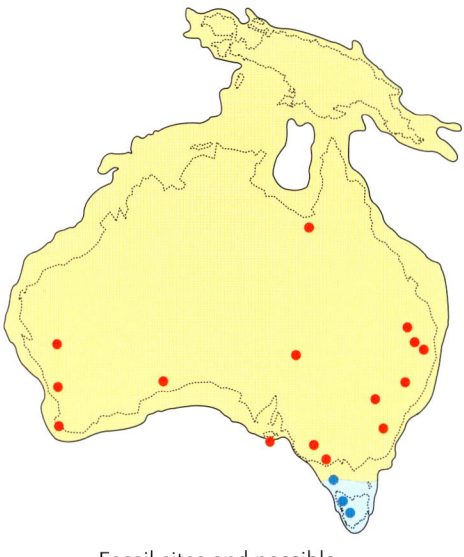

Fossil sites and possible distribution of
- 🔴 ⬜ *Zygomaturus trilobus*
- 🔵 ⬜ *Zygomaturus tasmanicus*

Zygomaturus trilobus was a large cow-sized relative of the diprotodons. It had long, strongly muscled legs and broad forepaws. *Zygomaturus* was certainly a herbivore and seems to have been restricted to the forested coastal fringes of the continent. Its remains are found in moister areas than *Diprotodon*, raising the possibility that it may have been aquatic, a bit like a small hippo. It may also have had a short trunk, like a tapir or elephant.

One of the most striking features of the *Zygomaturus* was its large head, most of which was filled with a complex network of sinuses. Large sinuses seem to be characteristic of large animals generally (including the diprotodons and *Palorchestes* as well as dinosaurs and modern large antelopes, for example) and could

PREHISTORIC GIANTS: THE MEGAFAUNA OF AUSTRALIA

have served many possible functions. Generally, however, it seems that large animals have large heads (perhaps because they need large mouths) which are heavy and so the complex air-filled sinal cavities are a way of lightening the skull without reducing its overall size or strength. *Zygomaturus* fossils found in Tasmania appear to belong to a different species to those found on the mainland, leading some scientists to regard *Zygomaturus tasmanicus* as separate from the mainland *Zygomaturus trilobus*.

The *Zygomaturus* skeleton in Museum Victoria is that of the smallest form, possibly *Zygomaturus tasmanicus*.

Palorchestes

CLASS: Mammalia
SUPERCOHORT: Marsupialia
ORDER: Diprotodontia
FAMILY: Palorchestidae

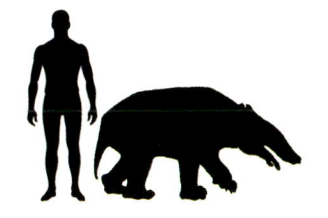

EXTINCT SPECIES		LENGTH	WEIGHT
Marsupial Tapir	*Palorchestes azeal*	2.00 m	500 kg
	Palorchestes parvus	1.20 m	100 kg
LIVING COMPARISON			
Malayan Tapir	*Tapirus indicus*	2.40 m	320 kg

For many years, scientists thought the strange bones of *Palorchestes azeal* belonged to a giant kangaroo. It wasn't until the 1950s that scientists suggested that these great beasts were more like the diprotodons than the kangaroos, and not until the 1970s that further fossil finds revealed just how strange and unusual these creatures really were.

Palorchestes was a broad-chested animal with smaller back legs and powerful curved forearms, each ending in large hooked claws. These long flattened claws, twelve centimetres long, were not necessarily for digging, but *Palorchestes* may have used them to rip branches or bark from trees. Its large, complex molars suggest that it fed on the fibrous plant material of the forests to which its fossils are restricted. It seems to have had a long thin tongue, which it may have used to grasp foliage, much as a giraffe does. Some reconstructions suggest that *Palorchestes* also had a trunk, another feature useful for pulling at foliage.

Both species of *Palorchestes* were relatively rare, suggesting that they occupied a highly specialised niche and were probably not social animals. The smaller *Palorchestes parvus* was much less common in the Pleistocene than it was in earlier times. Early members of this family seem to have been more widely distributed across the continent, but as the forests shrank to the eastern fringes, so too did the range of the great tree-ripper *Palorchestes*.

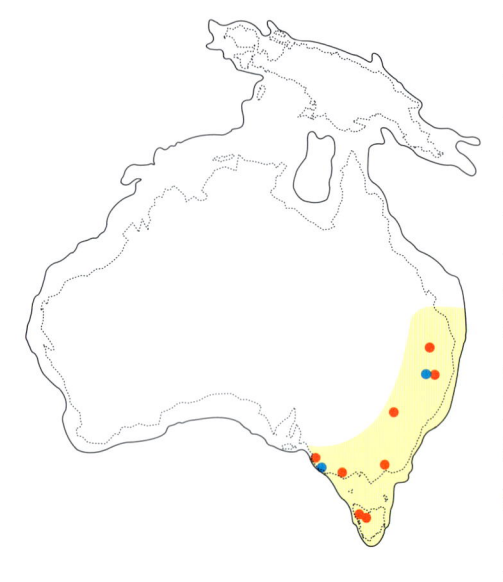

Fossil sites and possible distribution of
- ● ☐ *Palorchestes azeal*
- ● ☐ *Palorchestes parvus*

Megalibgwilia ramsayi

Monstrous monotremes, wombats and koalas

Not all Pleistocene giants were strange and unfamiliar creatures. Many looked very similar to the species we have today. The echidnas, wombats and koalas of the Pleistocene would all have been quite recognisable. But perhaps not many of us would want to get acquainted with a one metre long echidna or a wombat the size of a large sheep.

PREHISTORIC GIANTS: THE MEGAFAUNA OF AUSTRALIA

Echidnas

CLASS: Mammalia
ORDER: Monotremata
FAMILY: Tachyglossidae

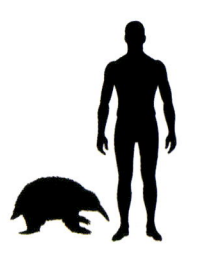

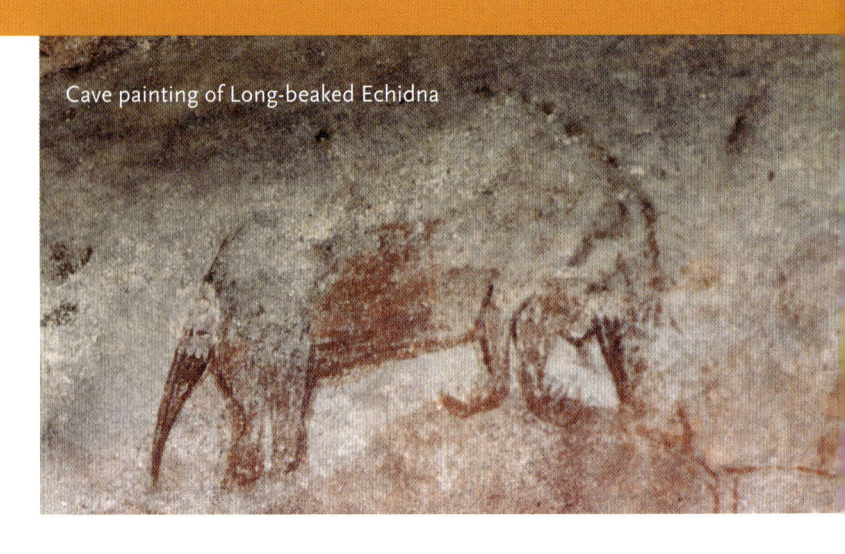

Cave painting of Long-beaked Echidna

EXTINCT SPECIES		LENGTH	WEIGHT
Giant Echidna	*Zaglossus hacketti*	0.80 m	30 kg
	Megalibgwilia ramsayi	0.55 m	10 kg
LIVING COMPARISON			
Short-beaked Echidna	*Tachyglossus aculeatus*	0.45 m	7 kg

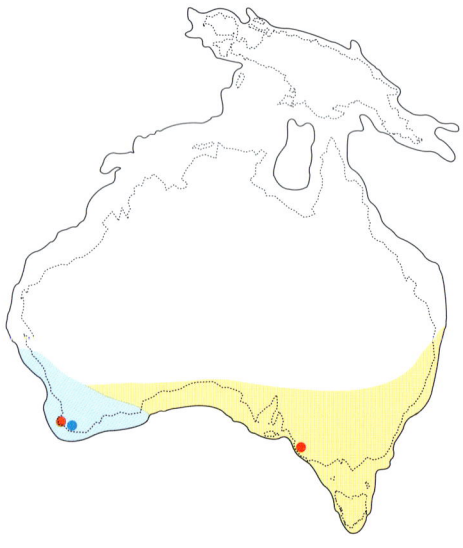

Fossil sites and possible distribution of
- *Zaglossus hacketti*
- *Megalibgwilia ramsayi*

The only living species of echidna in Australia today is the Short-beaked Echidna (*Tachyglossus aculeatus*), which grows to about the size of an overweight cat (but is much harder to pick up). But in the Pleistocene this tough little animal was ten percent bigger than it is today, and it had a couple of significantly larger relatives which were more than twice as big, and probably twice as tough too.

The giant Pleistocene echidnas were relatives of the long-beaked echidnas found in New Guinea. The modern Western Long-beaked Echidna (*Zaglossus bruijni*) is much bigger than the Australian species and eats a wider variety of invertebrates, including worms, instead of specialising in ants.

Fossil echidna remains are very rare in Australia and there are no complete skeletons but, from the fragments found at various sites, palaeontologists believe there were at least two other echidnas in the Pleistocene. *Megalibgwilia ramsayi* may not have been that much larger than the modern Short-beaked Echidna, but the Giant Echidna (*Zaglossus hacketti*) of Western Australia was a metre long—about the size of a modern wombat, but with spines. While you would not want to bump into one on a dark night, the Giant Echidna was probably just as harmless as its smaller modern cousins. Like the modern New Guinean species of long-beaked echidnas, it probably ate worms.

Scientists once dated the fossils of the smaller but more solidly built Robust Echidna (*Zaglossus robustus*) to the Pleistocene. However, re-dating of the gold-mine where the fossils were found has led scientists to think that the species was older, from the Miocene.

The skull of the Robust Echidna was originally thought to belong to a giant platypus. Despite their very different external appearance, platypus and echidna skulls can look very similar, and modern echidnas are surprisingly aquatic. But the platypus of the Pleistocene were pretty much identical to the modern species, and may well have formed an important part of Aboriginal diets in Tasmania during that time, judging from fossils found in caves inhabited by humans.

Long-beaked Echidna

PREHISTORIC GIANTS: THE MEGAFAUNA OF AUSTRALIA

Wombats

CLASS: Mammalia
ORDER: Monotremata
FAMILY: Tachyglossidae

EXTINCT SPECIES		LENGTH	WEIGHT
Giant Wombat	*Phascolonus gigas*	1.70 m	200 kg
Large Wombat	*Ramsayia magna*	1.30 m	100 kg
	Phascolomys medius	1.10 m	50 kg
	Vombatus hacketti	1.00 m	35 kg
LIVING COMPARISONS			
Common Wombat	*Vombatus ursinus*	0.98 m	26 kg

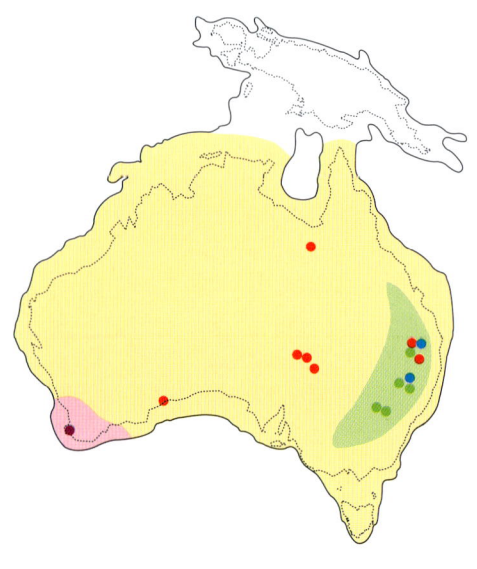

The Giant Wombat, *Phascolonus gigas*, was one of a number of fossil wombats described by Richard Owen at the British Museum in 1872. A few years later, the director of the South Australian Museum, Edward Stirling, and his colleagues found a more complete skull at Lake Callabonna. At twice the height and girth of the living Common Wombat, but with the same sturdy build and strong digging legs, the Giant Wombat must have been a formidable creature to encounter.

● □ ■ *Phascolonus gigas*   ● ■ *Phascolomys medius*
● ■ *Ramsayia magna*   ● ■ *Vombatus hacketti*

52

Palate of *Phascolonus gigas* from Lake Callabonna

Apart from their large size, Pleistocene wombats probably had very similar lives to modern wombats. They were grazers and probably dug for roots and tubers in forested areas, just like modern wombats do. While *Phascolonus gigas* appears to have been better adapted to grassland areas, the other wombats lived in woodland areas.

Modern wombats live in vast, complex warrens, but it is unlikely that wombats over about fifty kilograms could have done so. A burrow big enough for *Phascolonus gigas* would have been one metre in diameter, big enough for a child to walk inside standing upright. A long tunnel this size would collapse in most soil conditions. Other large mammals that utilise underground dens, like bears, tend to build simpler dens rather than complex warrens, and often utilise natural features such as fallen or hollow trees and rocks to support their dens. Grizzly Bears, for example (which are about the same size as the Giant Wombat), typically dig their dens about two metres into a slope, with a narrow entrance widening out into a bigger chamber.

Ramsayia magna was not quite as big as *Phascolonus gigas* but was probably still very much bigger than a modern wombat, while *Phascolomys medius* was only twice the size. Not all of the Pleistocene wombats were giants though. *Warendja wakefieldi* was a small, narrow-muzzled wombat found in western Victoria and South Australia which probably only grew to about half the size of modern wombats (about ten kilograms). Its slender form has led some scientists to suspect it may even have been able to climb trees.

Modern wombat

PREHISTORIC GIANTS: THE MEGAFAUNA OF AUSTRALIA

Koalas

CLASS: Mammalia
SUPERCOHORT: Marsupialia
ORDER: Diprotodontia
FAMILY: Phascolarctidae

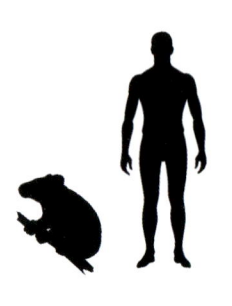

Miocene koala

EXTINCT SPECIES		LENGTH	WEIGHT
Giant Koala	*Phascolarctos stirtoni*	0.82 m	13 kg
LIVING COMPARISONS			
Koala	*Phascolarctos cinereus*	0.75 m	10 kg

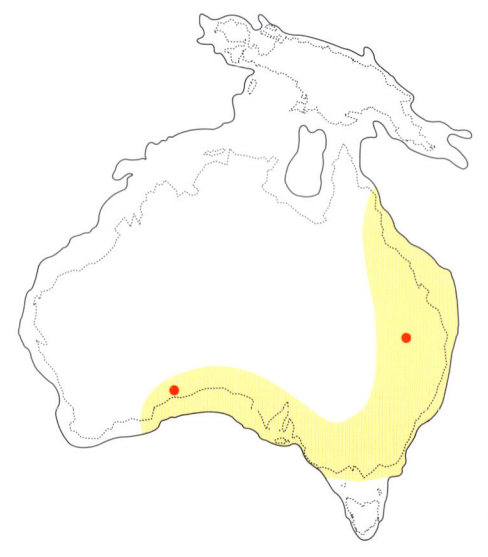

Fossil sites and distribution of Giant Koala

The Giant Koala (*Phascolarctos stirtoni*) was probably quite similar to its modern relative but larger by about almost one third. It may have averaged the size of the largest male koalas of today. Whilst not strictly a 'giant' it can probably be described as a robust koala. Both the modern and the extinct species co-existed during the Pleistocene and probably both lived in trees across a similar range. Like the modern Koala, the giants would certainly have been specialist gum-leaf browsers.

Despite its large size, the giant koala was not the largest member of its family. Earlier koalas were probably even larger. *Phascolarctos yorkensis*, from the Miocene period, was twice the size of the modern Koala. There were many other koala species in ancient Australia, but most of them were around the same size or smaller than the modern one.

Procoptodon goliah

Men of the forests and plains

Kangaroos have dominated the Australian landscape for millions of years, but in the Pleistocene, there were many species that looked quite different from the modern species. Kangaroos originated from small, possum-like animals, which descended from the trees about thirty million years ago (in the Oligocene) and adapted to life on the ground. They soon diversified into four families: the long-extinct Balbaridae kangaroos, the Hypsiprymnodontidae rat-kangaroos (which include the carnivorous Propleopine Rat-kangaroo described earlier), the potoroos (or Potoroidae) and the Macropodidae, which includes all the modern kangaroos and wallabies as well as several extinct groups. The most abundant of these extinct groups was the short-faced kangaroos or sthenurines.

PREHISTORIC GIANTS: THE MEGAFAUNA OF AUSTRALIA

Short-faced kangaroos

CLASS: Mammalia
SUPERCOHORT: Marsupialia
ORDER: Diprotodontia
FAMILY: Macropodidae
SUBFAMILY: Sthenurinae

GENUS	SPECIES	HEIGHT	WEIGHT
Procoptodon	*Procoptodon goliah*	2.60 m	232 kg
	Procoptodon williamsi	2.30 m	150 kg
	Procoptodon rapha	2.30 m	150 kg
	Procoptodon oreas	2.10 m	100 kg
	Procoptodon pusio	2.00 m	75 kg
	Procoptodon gilli	1.80 m	54 kg
	Procoptodon browneorum	1.70 m	50 kg
Simosthenurus	*Simosthenurus pales*	2.30 m	150 kg
	Simosthenurus occidentalis	2.20 m	118 kg
	Simosthenurus maddocki	2.00 m	78 kg
	Simosthenurus brachyselenis	2.00 m	70 kg
	Simosthenurus murrayi	2.00 m	70 kg
	Simosthenurus baileyi	1.80 m	55 kg
	Simosthenurus euryskaphus	1.80 m	55 kg
Metasthenurus	*Metasthenurus newtonae*	1.80 m	55 kg
Sthenurus	*Sthenurus stirlingi*	2.40 m	173 kg
	Sthenurus atlas	2.30 m	150 kg
	Sthenurus tindalei	2.30 m	127 kg
	Sthenurus andersoni	2.00 m	72 kg

LIVING COMPARISON

| Red Kangaroo | *Macropus rufus* | 1.90 m | 80 kg |

Eastern & Inland Distribution

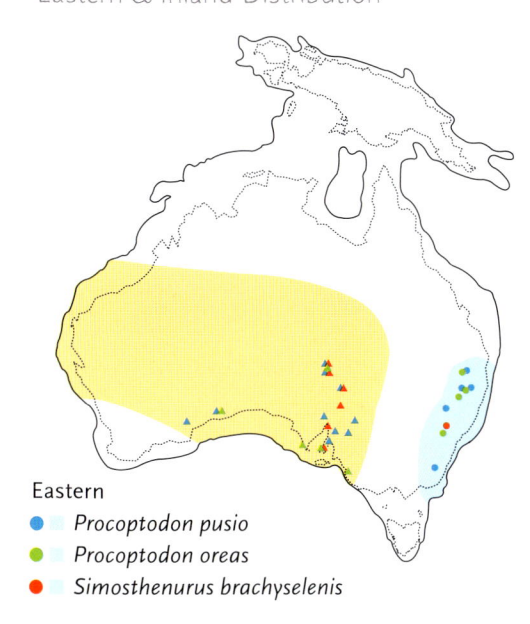

Eastern
- 🔵 ⬜ *Procoptodon pusio*
- 🟢 ⬜ *Procoptodon oreas*
- 🔴 ⬜ *Simosthenurus brachyselenis*

Inland
- 🔺 ⬜ *Sthenurus stirlingi*
- 🔺 ⬜ *Sthenurus tindalei*
- 🔺 ⬜ *Simosthenurus baileyi*

South-Eastern Distribution

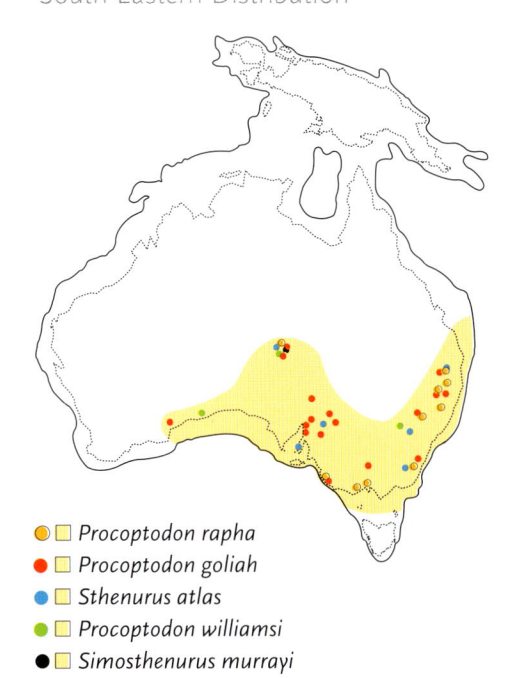

- 🟠 ⬜ *Procoptodon rapha*
- 🔴 ⬜ *Procoptodon goliah*
- 🔵 ⬜ *Sthenurus atlas*
- 🟢 ⬜ *Procoptodon williamsi*
- ⚫ ⬜ *Simosthenurus murrayi*

Southern Distribution

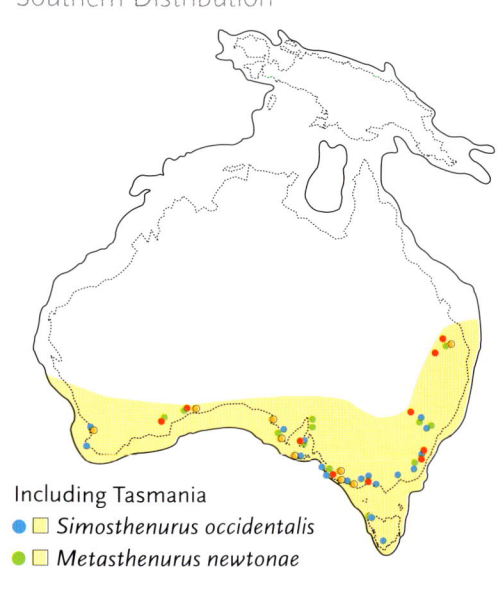

Including Tasmania
- 🔵 ⬜ *Simosthenurus occidentalis*
- 🟢 ⬜ *Metasthenurus newtonae*

Except Tasmania
- 🟠 ⬜ *Procoptodon browneorum*
- 🔴 ⬜ *Simosthenurus maddocki*

South & Widespread Distribution

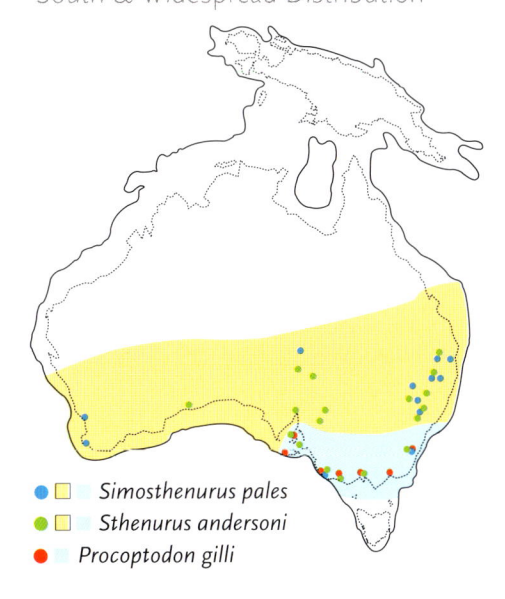

- 🔵 ⬜ *Simosthenurus pales*
- 🟢 ⬜ *Sthenurus andersoni*
- 🔴 ⬜ *Procoptodon gilli*

A *Sthenurus* kangaroo browsing on shrubs

Scientists once thought that the tiny Banded Hare-wallaby of the Western Australian islands in Shark Bay was the closest living link we had to the great mobs of short-faced kangaroos that once dominated the Australian landscape. This rare and secretive creature has similar teeth to some of the Pleistocene giants, but there the similarity ends. While the Banded Hare-wallaby is barely the size of a small cat, the sthenurine kangaroos were large, solidly built animals. The tallest, *Procoptodon goliah*, would have towered over the largest of the modern kangaroos.

Despite their hefty size, the sthenurines would have been fleet-footed animals. Like many fast runners (such as horses), they developed a single large toe with a hoof-like nail. This toe would have given them rapid acceleration at take-off and bursts of speed, although unlike modern kangaroos they seem not to have the build to sustain high speeds over a long distance.

Richard Owen named *Procoptodon goliah* after its distinctive teeth and large size. The genus is characterised by a short, deep skull with forward-facing eyes. Combined with their upright bipedal stance, this must have made procoptodons look surprisingly human—strange, furred 'men of the forest'. Like all sthenurines, the procoptodons were browsers, eating shrubs and bushes of the open woodlands rather than the dense rainforest. Their height would have been an advantage for a browser, enhanced by their bipedal upright stance and long arms. Their shoulder blades were similar to those of humans, allowing them to raise their arms above their heads to grasp foliage. And, like all sthenurines, procoptodons had two long hooked middle fingers, perhaps to help them pull branches down to their mouths. Their heavily enamelled and complex teeth had a multitude of fine ridges, suggesting that their food was rough and abrasive.

Simosthenurus is the genus that gives us the short-faced kangaroos. Although all sthenurines were characterised by shorter, deeper skulls compared to modern kangaroos, this feature is even more pronounced in this genus. Their short skulls would have had massive cheek muscles, giving these kangaroos an impressive bite and prodigious capacity to chew the dry, tough foliage of the expanding hard-leaved eucalypt and acacia forests that dominate Australia today. Teeth were not the only weapon with which to attack the foliage, however. *Simosthenurus maddocki* had much smaller teeth, and some scientists think it had a long manipulative tongue that it used, like a giraffe, to grasp leaves.

The *Sthenurus* genus is named after its robust tail, even though it was originally named from fragments of skull, teeth and jaw; a tail was not found until a century later. Like *Metasthenurus*, this genus had longer muzzles than the other short-faced kangaroos and their teeth seem to have been better adapted for feeding on the small-leaved saltbushes of the inland areas.

Ancient Aboriginal rock paintings of a kangaroo track with one big toe may be evidence of early contact between humans and sthenurines. In Western Australia, the legbone of a sthenurine was found with a notch that looked like it may have been made with a stone tool. Others bones appear to have been charred or smashed, which suggests they were cooked and then broken to extract the marrow. There seems little doubt that early Australians came face to face with these 'men of the forest' before they disappeared forever.

The extinct macropods

Class: Mammalia
Supercohort: Marsupialia
Order: Diprotodontia
Family: Macropodidae
Subfamily: Macropodinae

Protemnodon anak

PREHISTORIC GIANTS: THE MEGAFAUNA OF AUSTRALIA

EXTINCT SPECIES		HEIGHT	WEIGHT
	Protemnodon roechus	2.40 m	166 kg
	Protemnodon anak	2.25 m	131 kg
	Protemnodon brehus	2.15 m	110 kg
	Macropus ferragus	2.33 m	150 kg
	Macropus pearsoni	2.33 m	150 kg
	Congruus congruous	1.50 m	40 kg
	Macropus piltonensis	1.30 m	30 kg
	Macropus thor	1.30 m	30 kg
	Tropsodon minor	1.50 m	40 kg
	Wallabia kitcheneri	1.30 m	30 kg
LIVING COMPARISONS			
Black Wallaby	*Wallabia bicolor*	0.75 m	17 kg

The Pleistocene saw a great radiation of macropod kangaroos. Many were 'scaled-up' versions of the species we have today. Others, like the protemnodons, were unique to the Pleistocene and went extinct along with the short-faced kangaroos.

Fossils of *Protemnodon anak* occur across eastern Australia, including Tasmania and New Guinea, making it one of the most common Pleistocene species known. It had long arms, neck and muzzle, suggesting it may have stretched up into the foliage to feed. Skeletons have even been found with twigs and leaf fragments fossilised in the stomach region.

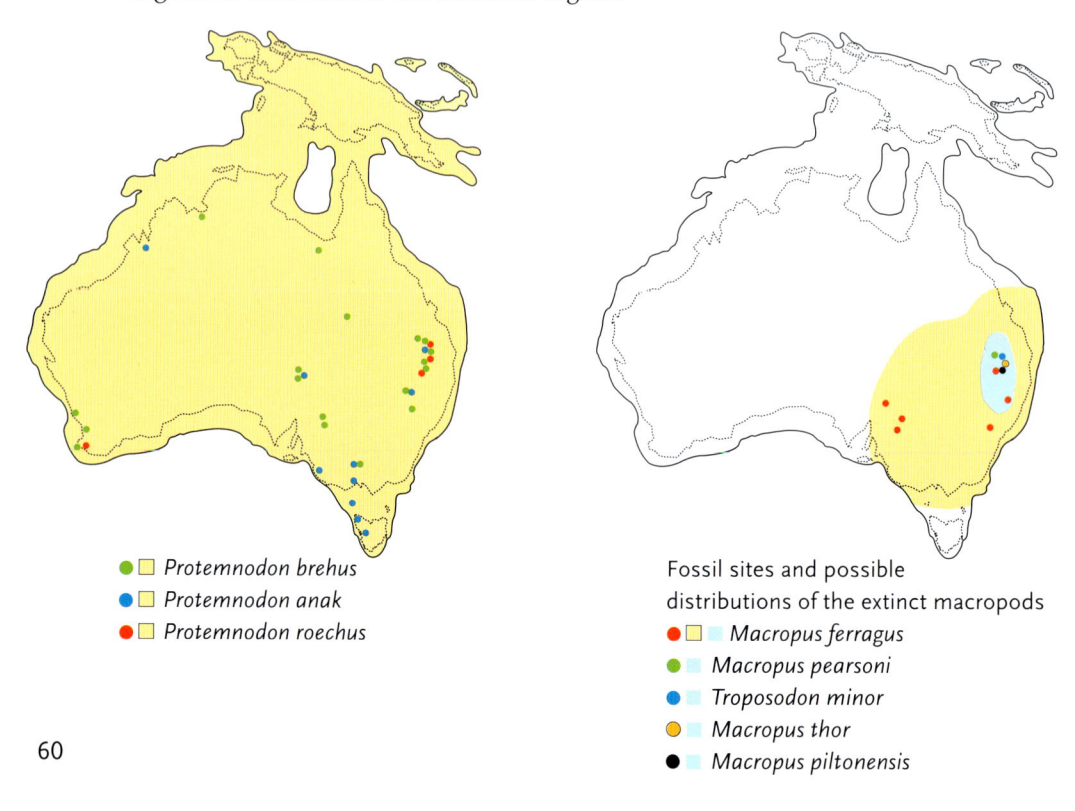

● □ *Protemnodon brehus*
● □ *Protemnodon anak*
● □ *Protemnodon roechus*

Fossil sites and possible distributions of the extinct macropods
● □ ■ *Macropus ferragus*
● ■ *Macropus pearsoni*
● ■ *Troposodon minor*
● ■ *Macropus thor*
● ■ *Macropus piltonensis*

The tiny Banded Hare-wallaby has similar teeth to the long extinct *Tropsodon minor*

The protemnodons clearly favoured the moist forest regions of the east coast, which, in the Pleistocene, continued north into New Guinea. Species unique to New Guinea included *Protemnodon hopei*, *Protemnodon nombe* and *Protemnodon tumbana*.

Tropsodon minor is named for its folded teeth—a trait it shares with the modern Banded Hare-wallaby (*Lagostrophus fasciatus*). This has led to both *Tropsodon minor* and the Banded Hare-wallaby being classified as sthenurines, but the latest taxonomic research suggests that they are both either macropods or a separate lineage of kangaroos altogether. *Tropsodon minor* was a widespread species along the east coast, with fossils occurring throughout Queensland, New South Wales and Victoria.

A great variety of fossil *Macropus* species have been found at late Pleistocene sites, including Darling Downs, Lancefield, Naracoorte and Wellington Caves. Many of them, however, are known only from one or two specimens, making it difficult to describe them as species. Only the more established species are listed on page 60, but many others are likely to come to light as further research is completed. Many of the larger *Macropus* species, like *Macropus ferragus* and *Macropus pearsoni*, also went extinct in the Pleistocene. But many other *Macropus* giants didn't so much disappear, as shrink into the modern forms we are familiar with today.

PREHISTORIC GIANTS: THE MEGAFAUNA OF AUSTRALIA

Modern kangaroos

CLASS: Mammalia
SUPERCOHORT: Marsupialia
ORDER: Diprotodontia
FAMILY: Macropodidae
SUBFAMILY: Macropodinae

Red Kangaroo

Red Kangaroo

DWARFED SPECIES	PLEISTOCENE FORM > MODERN FORM	LENGTH	WEIGHT
Red Kangaroo	*Macropus rufus*	2.40 m	115 kg
	> *Macropus rufus*	1.80 m	85 kg
Eastern Grey Kangaroo	*Macropus giganteus titan*	2.60 m	86 kg
	> *Macropus giganteus*	2.00 m	66 kg
Common Wallaroo	*Macropus robustus altus*	2.40 m	57 kg
	> *Macropus robustus*	1.90 m	47 kg
Agile Wallaby	*Macropus siva*	0.90 m	22 kg
	> *Macropus agilis*	0.80 m	19 kg
Swamp Wallaby	*Wallabia vishnu*	0.90 m	20 kg
	> *Wallabia bicolor*	0.80 m	17 kg

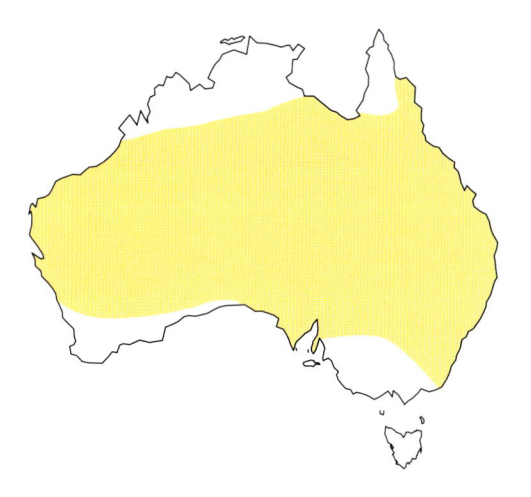

Modern distribution of the Common Wallaroo *Macropus robustus*

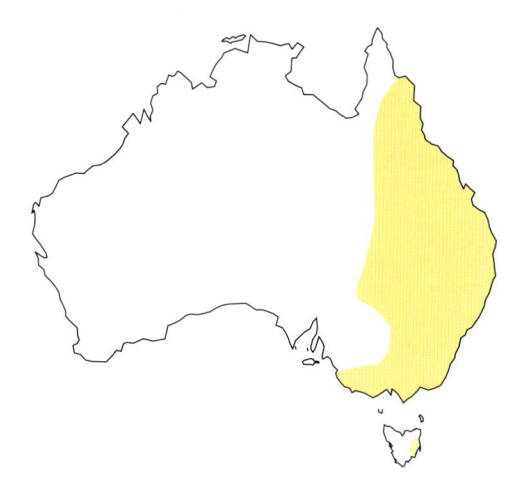

Modern distribution of the Eastern Grey Kangaroo *Macropus giganteus*

The fossil taxonomy of the modern kangaroos is poorly understood and complicated by the fact that many fossil forms are the same as living species, or much larger versions of living species. This has led to a proliferation of names, often from a small sample of fossils.

Macropus kangaroos differ from the other kangaroos of the Pleistocene because they include specialist grazers, which were well suited to the changing climate and expanding grasslands of the Australian interior. These are the kangaroos we are familiar with in Australia today.

Yet despite their success and survival into the modern era, macropod kangaroos did not escape the Pleistocene extinction unscathed. While some species went extinct, many others dramatically reduced in size. The fossil form of the Grey Kangaroo, *Macropus giganteus titan*, was twice the size of its modern descendant, yet otherwise is clearly the same species. It seems likely, therefore, that the giant form probably had a similar lifestyle to the modern species. It certainly favoured open woodlands of the east coast, perhaps using them for shelter during the day and emerging onto the grasslands to graze at night, gathering in large numbers.

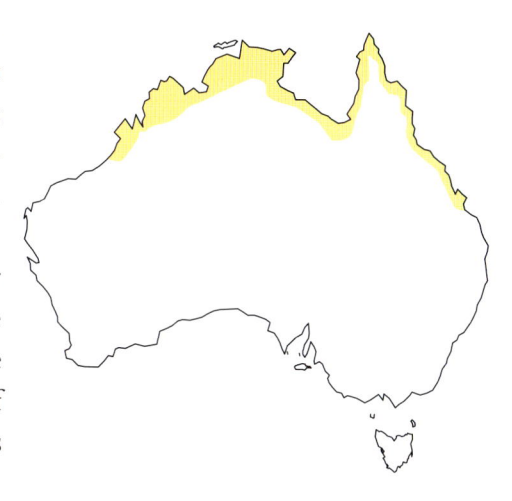

Modern distribution of the Agile Wallaby *Macropus agilis*

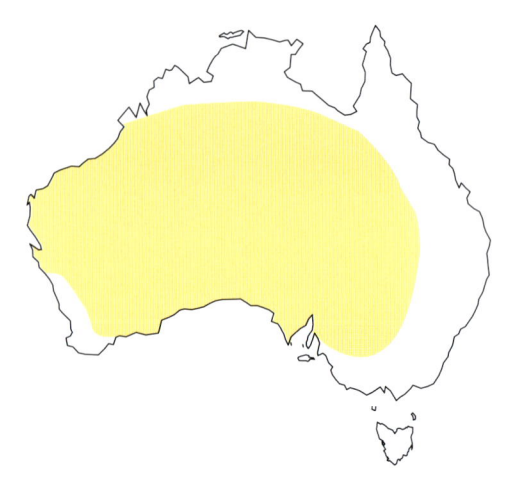

PREHISTORIC GIANTS: THE MEGAFAUNA OF AUSTRALIA

Modern distribution of the Red Kangaroo *Macropus rufus*

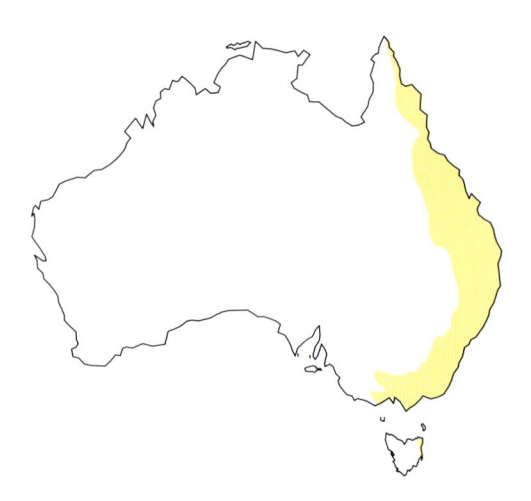

Modern distribution of the Swamp Wallaby *Wallabia bicolor*

Similarly, the solidly built *Macropus birdselli* may have been a large Euro or Common Wallaroo (*Macropus robustus*), a rather shaggy-looking, heavy kangaroo found right across inland Australia, excluding the south coast and northern tips of the continent. Common Wallaroos have a characteristically large black nose, and the darker males are usually twice the size of the females. They are solitary animals, only socialising during the mating season or when they have young at foot.

The delicate build of *Macropus siva* suggests a close affinity with the Agile Wallaby *Macropus agilis*. Both are restricted to the northern region of Australia and lowlands of New Guinea. Modern Agile Wallabies are nervy creatures that graze on the grasslands of rivers and streams in large groups. Like the Wallaroo, they are sexually dimorphic, with the males being considerably larger than the females.

The only surviving member of the *Wallabia* genus today is the Swamp or Black Wallaby (*Wallabia bicolor*), which has eleven chromosomes in males and ten in females—unlike other modern wallabies, with sixteen chromosomes. The fossil *Wallabia vishnu* is remarkably similar to the modern Swamp Wallaby but twice its size. Fossils from the early Pliocene have been found in south-eastern Queensland, suggesting that the Swamp Wallaby, like many other modern kangaroos, only escaped the Pleistocene extinction by dwarfing.

Grey Kangaroos are among the largest surviving macropods today

Eastern Grey Kangaroo

Extinction

Rock art painting of Thylacine

Why did the megafauna disappear? This question has pre-occupied scientists ever since 1796, when Georges Cuvier declared that fossil elephants from northern Europe were indisputably different from the modern elephants found in Africa and Asia. The existence of extinct species quite distinct from those found today proved to Cuvier 'the existence of a world previous to ours, destroyed by some kind of catastrophe.'

The unfortunate frozen mammoths, miraculously preserved in an icy death, symbolised for Cuvier the sudden cataclysmic nature of extinctions generally. Through his study of the geological layers in the earth and their relationships with the different types of animals found in each layer, Cuvier proposed that life had been extinguished and re-appeared five times during Earth's history. Cuvier believed this had happened suddenly, and religious figures took this argument as evidence of biblical catastrophes such as the great flood.

While most earlier extinctions appear to have taken place over a long period of time and are thought to have been the result of gradual climate changes or the after-effects of asteroid impacts, the Pleistocene extinctions occurred over a much shorter period of time. And they coincided, in many instances, with the spread of humans around the world. This has led to much speculation and debate about the role humans have played in Pleistocene extinctions, both globally and on different land masses.

The circumstantial evidence against humans is striking. Wherever humans went, megafauna disappeared. The only places megafauna have survived in any numbers are in the oceans and in Africa, where humans first evolved (and where the wildlife has had a long time to grow accustomed to their hunting habits). We know modern humans have a long track record of causing extinctions and rapidly depleting native species. But is this a feature of our species, evidenced from our earliest interactions with the natural world? Or are suspicions about human involvement in Pleistocene extinctions just a case of a suspect with prior convictions being in the wrong place at the wrong time?

Many scientists believe that other factors contributed to the Pleistocene extinctions. Some North American researchers believe that humans could not have wiped out the megafauna as quickly as they appear to have disappeared and that some other factor such as disease must have been the cause. In Australia the paucity of Pleistocene fossil sites and the difficulty dating them makes it hard to establish how quickly species went extinct. While there seems to be some evidence of humans eating megafauna, other scientists argue that humans may not even have co-existed with megafauna. The gradually changing climate in the late Pleistocene certainly altered the landscape for many species, but whether such changes were enough to drive species to extinction is difficult to say.

Extinction is nearly always caused by a multiplicity of factors. Some species seem very vulnerable to extinction. Highly specialised species, dependant on very particular environments or food are often unable to adapt to changes to their environment. Long-lived, slow-breeding species also have little time to adapt. Rare species or small isolated populations are more likely to be wiped out by an unfortunate cataclysm than species that are more abundant or widespread. And species that have been around for longer also seem to be more vulnerable to extinction.

Yet other species we cannot extinguish no matter how hard we try. Humans have waged untold wars on a multitude of invertebrates and bacteria with little or no success. We have mercilessly hunted pest species and invested millions of dollars on eradication programs for feral animals, to no avail. These species tend to be short-lived, rapid-breeding generalists, able to adapt rapidly and successfully to environmental changes and to whatever new weapons humans hurl at them.

Even when humans clearly are implicated in the eradication of a species, hunting alone is rarely the only cause. European colonists certainly hunted the Thylacine to extinction in Tasmania, but the Thylacine had already disappeared from the mainland long before Europeans arrived. This earlier extinction seems not to have been caused directly by humans, but indirectly by the arrival of the Dingo in Australia.

Similarly, hunting was not directly responsible for driving the gentle Bilby (*Macrotis lagotis*) to near-extinction and its cousin the Lesser Bilby (*Macrotis leucura*) to oblivion, but that does not mean humans were not involved. Certainly introduced cats and foxes took a significant toll on bilbies, but competition with introduced rabbits was perhaps just as important. Rabbits changed the vegetation, just as humans did through agriculture, land clearing, grazing and the introduction of pastures and exotic weeds. Fire regimes also changed, fundamentally altering the vegetation. All of these things placed additional pressure on bilby populations, which were already fragmented and isolated prior to European colonisation.

Thus, the lesson to be learnt from the extinction of the megafauna does not relate to whether humans hunted them to extinction (suddenly or gradually) or whether climate change was to blame, or whether one or other of these factors changed the vegetation pattern or a combination of all of the above. We cannot answer that question for species whose extinction we have witnessed, documented and studied intensively, let alone ones that disappeared thousands of years ago and whose life histories we know precious little about.

The message worth taking home is that some species are more vulnerable to environmental change than others. Large species, slow-breeding species, specialist species and isolated species are all vulnerable to extinction when their environment changes. And the one feature that characterises humans above all else is their remarkable ability to change the environment, whether intentionally or not. Humans may or may not have been responsible for the extinction of the megafauna, but the fate of a great many other, equally fascinating species, rests in our hands today. And it is up to us to make sure they do not also disappear, leaving nothing more than footsteps and fossils in the future.

FURTHER INFORMATION

Museums

Museum Victoria, Carlton Gardens, Melbourne VIC

Tasmania Museum and Art Gallery, Hobart TAS

Queen Victoria Museum and Art Gallery, Launceston TAS

South Australian Museum, Adelaide SA

Western Australian Museum, Perth WA

Museum of Central Australia, Alice Springs NT

Queensland Museum, South Bank, Brisbane QLD

Australian Museum, Hyde Park, Sydney NSW

Fossil sites

Buchan Caves Reserve, Parks Victoria VIC

Wonambi Fossil Centre, Naracoorte Caves National Park SA

Mammoth Cave, Margaret River WA

Wellington Caves, Wellington, NSW

Riversleigh Fossil Centre, Mt Isa QLD

Books

Johnson, C 2006, *Australia's mammal extinctions: A 50 000 year history*, Cambridge University Press, Melbourne.

Long, J, Archer, M, Flannery T and Hand S 2002, *Prehistoric mammals of Australia and New Guinea*, University of New South Wales Press, Sydney.

Molnar, RE 2004, *Dragons in the dust: the paleobiology of the giant monitor lizard Megalania*, Indiana University Press, Bloomington.

Murray, PF and Vickers-Rich, P 2004, *Magnificent Mihirungs: The colossal flightless birds of the Australian Dreamtime*, Indiana University Press, Bloomington.

Rich, PV, van Tets, GF and Knight, F 1985, *Kadimakara: Extinct vertebrates of Australia*, Pioneer Design Studios, Melbourne.

Websites

Prehistoric Life (Museum Victoria)
www.museumvictoria.com.au/prehistoric/mammals/australia.html

Oz Fossils (ABC)
www.abc.net.au/science/ozfossil/megafauna/

Australian Beasts (ABC)
www.abc.net.au/science/ausbeasts/

The Bonediggers (PBS)
www.pbs.org/wgbh/nova/bonediggers/

Australia's Lost Kingdoms (Australian Museum)
www.lostkingdoms.com/

Wonambi Fossil Centre (SA Department for Environment and Heritage)
www.parks.sa.gov.au/naracoorte/wonambi/index.htm

Megadig (Museum of Central Australia)
archive.amol.org.au/discovernet/alcoota/museum.asp

AUTHOR'S BIOGRAPHY

Danielle Clode is a zoologist and science writer at the University of Melbourne with a particular interest in the history of Australian zoology. She has a doctorate in animal behaviour from Oxford University and has worked as a scientific interpreter, essayist and research fellow at Museum Victoria. Danielle is the author of several books, including *Continent of Curiosities* (2006), inspired by the collections and curators at Museum Victoria, and *Voyages to the South Seas* (2007), about French scientific expeditions to Australia.

ACKNOWLEDGEMENTS

I would like to thank Melanie Raymond and Robin Hirst for co-ordinating, overseeing and supporting this project. The expert advice and assistance of John Long, Tom Rich, Bill Birch, Paul Willis and Ben Kear has been invaluable. Sandra Winchester, Wayne Longmore and Ingrid Unger provided advice and assistance with collections of articles, animals and images respectively. David Meagher provided an editorial overview. Thanks are also due to Matthew Cupper, Stephen Gallagher, David Pickering, Gilbert Price, Ralph Molnar, Wayne Gertz and Stephen Carey for their assistance with megafaunal discussions. Finally, I would like to dedicate this book to my late supervisor, Dr Frank Dalziel (1935–1999), who inspired generations of psychology students at Adelaide University with his enthusiasm for studying 'the behaviour of dead animals'. I hope this book helps continue that tradition.

The museum was fortunate to receive permission to reproduce the Megafauna images from the 2008 October Stamp Collecting Month issue. The images were commissioned by Australia Post, the copyright owner, and the works were created by artist, Peter Trusler. The scientific consultants were Prof. Patricia Vickers-Rich, Prof. Rod Wells, Dr Peter Murray, Dr Thomas Rich and Aaron Camens. Museum Victoria also wishes to thank Bruce Davidson, Mary Hoban and Michael Zsolt of Australia Post for allowing us to reproduce these images.

PICTURE CREDITS

ii   Footsteps from a member of the Diprotontidae family, found in the Western District, Victoria. Photographer: Peter Swinkels

vi   *Meiolania platyceps* skeleton. Photographer: J. Fields. Courtesy Australian Museum. Also page 34

viii-1   Megafauna. Artist: Peter Trusler. Courtesy Australia Post*

5   Late Pleistocene vegetation map

7   Based on a timeline created by David Meagher

11   The Buchan Caves. Photographer: Rodney Start

12   Plan of Large and Bone Caves, Wellington, New South Wales, 1830. Created by Thomas Mitchell. Source: National Library of Australia

13   Large Cavern at Wellington Valley. Major T.L. Mitchell del.; Day & Haghe lithrs. Published 1839. Source: National Library of Australia

15   Fossil bones from Thylacoleo Cave in Western Australia. Photographer: John Long

16   Kangaroo footprints from the Pleistocene, Western District, Victoria. Photographer: Peter Swinkels. Source: Museum Victoria

18   *Thylacine* rock art. Photographer: George Chaloupka

19   *Thylacinus cyanocephalus* (detail). Artist: Peter Trusler. Courtesy Australia Post*

20   *Thylacoleo carnifex* (detail). Artist: Peter Trusler. Courtesy Australia Post*

21   *Thylacoleo carnifex*. Artist: Frank Knight. From P. V. Rich and G. van Tets, *Kadimakara*. Copyright P. Vickers-Rich.

22   *Thylacoleo* skeletons from Nullabor caves. Photographer: John Long

22   *Thylacinus cyanocephalus*. Artist: John Gould, *The Mammals of Australia*, 1863, plate 5.

23   Thylacine at Beaumaris Zoo, Hobart. Courtesy of the Tasmanian Museum and Art Gallery

24   *Propleopus oscillans*. Artist: Frank Knight. From P. V. Rich and G. van Tets, *Kadimakara*. Copyright P. Vickers-Rich.

26   *Megalania prisca* (detail). Artist: Peter Trusler. Courtesy Australia Post*

27   *Megalania prisca*. Artist: Peter Trusler

28   *Megalania* skeletal reconstruction. Photographer: Michelle McFarlane. Source: Museum Victoria

29   *Quinkana fortirostrum*. Artist: Frank Knight. From P. V. Rich and G. van Tets, *Kadimakara*. Copyright P. Vickers-Rich.

31   Saltwater crocodile. Source: National Archives of Australia 591/08 NAA-11678685_1

31   *Wonambi naracoortensis*. Artist: Frank Knight. From P. V. Rich and G. van Tets, *Kadimakara*. Copyright P. Vickers-Rich.

32   *Wonambi* fossil. Photographer: David John Barrie

33   *Meiolania platyceps*. Artist: Frank Knight. From P. V. Rich and G. van Tets, *Kadimakara*. Copyright P. Vickers-Rich.

35   *Genyornis newtoni* (detail). Artist: Peter Trusler. Courtesy Australia Post*

36   *Genyornis newtoni*. Artist: Frank Knight. From P. V. Rich and G. van Tets, *Kadimakara*. Copyright P. Vickers-Rich.

37   Mihirung and emu comparison. Artist: Peter Murray

38   Giant Malleefowl. Artist: Frank Knight. From P. V. Rich and G. van Tets, *Kadimakara*. Copyright P. Vickers-Rich.

39   Giant Coucal. Artist: Frank Knight. From P. V. Rich and G. van Tets, *Kadimakara*. Copyright P. Vickers-Rich.

41   *Diprotodon* (detail). Artist: Peter Trusler. Courtesy Australia Post*

42   *Diprotodon*. Artist: Frank Knight. From P. V. Rich and G. van Tets, *Kadimakara*. Copyright P. Vickers-Rich.

43   *Diprotodon* skeleton. Photographer: John Broomfield. Source: Museum Victoria

44   *Diprotodon* skull. Photographer: Rodney Start. Source: Museum Victoria

45   *Zygomaturus*. Artist: Peter Schouten

46   *Zygomaturus* skeleton. Photographer: Benjamin Healley. Source: Museum Victoria

47   *Palorchestes*. Artist: Frank Knight. From P. V. Rich and G. van Tets, *Kadimakara*. Copyright P. Vickers-Rich.

49   Long-beaked Echidna. Artist: Anne Musser

50   Rock art painting of Long-beaked Echidna. Photographer: George Chaloupka

51   Long-beaked Echidna. Photographers: David Parer & Elizabeth Parer-Cook

52   Wombat. Artist: Peter Schouten

53   Modern wombat. Photographer: Mark Pulford

53 Palate of *Phascolonus gigas*. Photographer: John Long. Courtesy of the South Australia Museum

54 Giant koala. Artist: Anne Musser

55 *Procoptodon goliah* (detail). Artist: Peter Trusler. Courtesy Australia Post*

56 *Sthenurus* kangaroo. Artist: Frank Knight. From P. V. Rich and G. van Tets, *Kadimakara*. Copyright P. Vickers-Rich.

58 *Sthenurus* kangaroo. Artist: Peter Murray

59 *Protemnodon anak*. Artist: Peter Murray

61 Banded Hare-Wallaby. Artist: John Gould, *The Mammals of Australia*, Vol.2, 1863, plate 56

62 Red Kangaroo. Photographer: Lindy Lumsden

62 Red Kangaroo. Artist: John Gould, *The Mammals of Australia*, Vol.2, 1863, plate 6

64 Eastern Grey Kangaroo. Photographer: Lindy Lumsden

65 Eastern Grey Kangaroo. Artist: John Gould, *The Mammals of Australia*, Vol.2, 1863, plate 1

66 Rock art painting of Thylacine. Photographer: George Chaloupka

* This material has been reproduced with permission of the Australian Postal Corporation. The original work is held in the National Philatelic Collection.

Maps primarily sourced from *Kadimakara: Extinct vertebrates of Australia*, edited by P. Vickers Rich, G. van Tets and F. Wright, 1985, and *Quaternary Extinctions: A prehistoric revolution* edited by P. S. Martin and R. G. Klein, 1984. The silhouettes were supplied by and reproduced with the permission of the Naracoorte Caves National Park. The Sthenurus maps are based on *Systematics and Evolution of the Sthenurine Kangaroos* by G. Prideaux, 2004. Additional details sourced from scientific articles.